Dedication

I dedicate this work to my wife, Rachel, who is my daily prayer mate; and to those who have known and walked with me through much of my pilgrim journey on this earth in which I have sought to "know Him and the power of His resurrection"—my late wife, Ecke, who stood by my side for over 50 years; my daughter, Judi Trimble, and son-in-love, John; and my son, Stephen, with his lovely wife, Alaina.

The family moved from place to place with me, suffering with me in accusations and stresses of church life. They watched as I struggled to be husband, daddy, and pastor all at the same time.

There are others, such as the Robinsons, Mooneyhams, Sisks, Kollmanns, and Castons, who suffered hardship as we went to and through the desert of Arizona, both physically and spiritually. There we began to learn that intimacy with Christ was more important than material things.

Others also, too numerous to mention, prayed for me and stood by me when they did not fully understand what it was that I was doing.

To all the above, some who have gone on to be with their Bridegroom, I affectionately, sincerely, and humbly dedicate these pages.

Recommendation

*An **Invitation To Intimacy*** is a challenge to move from being God influenced to being God possessed. Only intimacy will produce Bride consciousness, Bride passion, and Bride readiness. Jesus is coming for a Bride, not an institution. As no one I have read, Millard Box has brought the cryptic and mysterious *Song of Solomon* to clarity as an invitation to intimacy between the believer and the Lover Lord.

Few have had occasion to delve where Millard has gone. He has dared to follow the Lord where few, if any, understood. He exemplifies "bringing fruit in old age." His life and this work, *An Invitation To Intimacy*, are residual challenges to the body of Christ in general and believers in particular to develop Bride consciousness through intimacy.

I recommend this work to all serious believers and even to those who may not be as serious as they desire to be.

Jack Taylor
Dimension Ministries
Indianatlantic, Florida

SOLOMON'S SONG OF SONGS

An Invitation to Intimacy

Illustrating the maturing
of the bride of Christ.

Dr. Millard B. Box

LAURUS BOOKS

Unless otherwise notated, all Scripture references are from the King James Version of the Holy Bible, available in the Public Domain.

Scripture quotations marked (NKJV) are taken from the New King James Version®. Copyright © 1982 by Thomas Nelson, Inc. Used by permission. All rights reserved.

Scripture quotations marked (AMP) are taken from the Amplified® Bible, Copyright © 1954, 1958, 1962, 1964, 1965, 1987 by The Lockman Foundation. Used by permission.)

Scripture quotations marked (DT) are from the Darby Translation, available in the Public Domain.

An Invitation to Intimacy

Dr. Millard B. Box

Copyright © 2014 by Millard B. Box

All rights reserved. This book is protected under the copyright laws of the United States of America. This book may not be copied or reprinted for commercial gain or profit. The use of short quotations or occasional page copying for personal or group study is permitted and encouraged. Permission will be granted on request.

Paperback: ISBN: 978-1-938526-83-1

ePub (iBooks, Nook): ISBN: 978-1-938526-84-8

Mobi (Kindle): ISBN: 978-1-938526-85-5

Published by LAURUS BOOKS

LAURUS BOOKS
P.O. Box 894
Locust Grove, GA 30248 USA
www.TheLaurusCompany.com

This book may be purchased in paperback from TheLaurusCompany.com, Amazon.com, and other retailers around the world. Also available in formats for electronic readers from their respective stores.

Foreword

It was by a directive from the Lord that I began to study the *Song of Solomon* several years ago. Through these years, I have continued to expand my understanding of what God is saying in this book. A little time ago, as I preached through the book to the congregation of Life Church, and as I taught the book to students in a college in Kiev, Ukraine, I was directed to write the words that follow. I pray that you will find an intimacy with God the Father, Son, and Holy Spirit in your perusal of these pages.

When one thinks of the men who were used of the Holy Spirit to pen the thoughts of God, seldom do we consider Solomon. If "all Scripture" is given by inspiration and men "divinely moved" wrote those Scriptures, then Solomon must be one of them, just as John or Matthew or Paul. I sense a "shrug of the shoulders" by theologians when it comes to the interpretation of this book. However, the *Song of Solomon* is much more than a poem or history or philosophical treatise. When this book has been studied and presented for consideration to the student of the Bible, all sorts of "theories" have been proposed. I will not waste your time or mine by listing

FOREWORD

them or giving them credence.

All of the content in the Word of God is important because there is not a word or syllable without meaning when taught by the Author, the Holy Spirit. Not one jot or tittle will pass away, our Lord said, until all be fulfilled. Therefore, an in-depth study will do us no harm, and the wonderful Spirit of God will have opportunity to draw us nearer to the Bridegroom as we read and study.

I cannot prove what I am going to say, but I sincerely believe that God chose this man Solomon to write in cryptic language with symbolisms that reveal the Lord Jesus Christ and the individual believer in their walk together in fellowship and love.

Study Outline

Introduction 9
  Song of Solomon 1:1

  I. Intimacy Commenced *(First Love)* 13
  Song of Solomon 1:2 – 2:7

 II. Intimacy Conflicted *(Faltering Love)* 47
  Song of Solomon 2:8 – 3:5

III. Intimacy Communicated *(Flourishing Love)* 65
  Song of Solomon 3:6 – 5:1

IV. Intimacy Concentrated *(Forming [Transforming] Love)* ... 97
  Song of Solomon 5:2 – 7:13

 V. Intimacy Consummated *(Finished [Mature] Love)* 141
  Song of Solomon 8:1-14

About the Author 157

From the publisher: I was most blessed to have been in attendance when Dr. Box expounded upon this cherished and often misunderstood Book a few years ago when we attended church together. His revelatory teaching on the Song of Solomon was truly eye opening and life changing, not only provoking those who heard it to a more mature and intimate relationship with our Lord and heavenly Bridegroom, but to study all of God's Word with fresh Spirit-led understanding.

We at The Laurus Company and Laurus Books are honored to present this powerful teaching. May all those who open this book be enriched with the reading.

—Nancy E. Williams, President
The Laurus Company

Introduction

Jesus referred twice to Solomon's glory and wisdom. Matthew 6:29: *"and yet I say to you that even Solomon in all his glory was not arrayed like one of these."* Jesus was speaking of the lilies of the field. We will speak of the lilies and their meaning farther along in this book. Jesus spoke of Solomon the second time when He said in Matthew 12:42: *"The queen of the South will rise up in judgment with this generation and condemn it, for she came from the ends of the earth to hear the wisdom of Solomon; and indeed a greater than Solomon is here."*

Solomon's two birth names indicate his authorship. One name was Solomon, which means "peace," and the other is Jedidiah, which means "love." He, in this song, personifies the covenant love of the Lord. You, represented by the Shulamite maiden, depict the covenant love bride of the Lord Jesus Christ.

There is as much symbolism in this as there is in the book of *Revelation*. So I do not intend to make each and every word mean something. I believe I shall be led of the Holy Spirit of God to explain these passages in order to bring you into an intimate relationship with the Bridegroom. I do not mean these writings to be a theological work wherein we study *about* the Lord, but the intent here is for us to see a picture of the Master as your Bridegroom and for you to love Him more each moment.

Jesus, the Messiah, is pictured here as Shepherd-King and is portrayed in that role throughout the book. The Hebrews called this writing "The Book of Communion" and the "Holy of Holies." They read or chanted portions of this writing as they worshiped the God of heaven and earth. The reason, I am told, is that they regarded God as the husband of Israel and they worshiped Him as such.

The Song of Solomon is a mirror of the glorified Lord, so that we, *"beholding in a glass the glory of the Lord, be transformed into the same image, from glory to glory"* (2 Corinthians 3:18). The book is veiled in language understood only by the one whose spirit loves and seeks the Lord. A nominal Christian, whether teacher, professor, language expert, or theologian "par excellence," cannot understand what the Holy Spirit is saying merely by intellectual acumen. Just because I know the Hebrew text does not make me an expert in interpretation of any passage in the Old Testament any more than knowing how to mix paint makes me an artist. The same is true of the Greek language in interpretation of the New Testament. I do not decry this basis for study of the Bible. But to assume you know what God is saying based merely on the merits of interpretative logic is to miserably fail. Love is the key to understanding and knowing this lovely book. If you, deep in your heart, do not genuinely love Him and "pant" for Him as the deer pants for the water, you will never understand what He is saying to you. It is taught only, as all Scripture, by the Author, the Holy Spirit, to your spirit first. Otherwise, *Song of Solomon* becomes doctrinal, historical, poetical, or even carnal.

This book is the heart history of the saint who seeks a closer walk and union with the heavenly Bridegroom. This writing, embedded in the Old Testament writings, shows your Lord leading you by love ever closer to fellowship with Him. He woos you from one degree to another until His image is stamped on your life and your face. When two people are in love, it cannot be hidden. There is an "aura" about them that, try as they may, cannot be kept secret. Oh, that this were true about us with Him. It is said that when one preacher, many years ago, walked into a room, people fell under conviction and came to the Lord. He walked with Jesus so closely that the "aura" was detectable even by men who did not know the Lord in salvation. The only way this is attained is by "falling in love" with our Lord Jesus Christ.

There is picture language, symbols, dreams, visions, etc., used by the Holy Spirit in all the Bible. Approach this *Song* in reverence and holy expectancy. Permit the precious Bridegroom to draw you ever nearer to Him. Forget your bias and prejudice and religious knowledge. Just relax and seek Him. In verse one (1:1), the *Song of Solomon* is called a love song of all love songs. Solomon composed one thousand and five

(1,005) songs. First Kings 4:32: *"And he spake three thousand [3,000] proverbs and his songs were one thousand and five"* (bracketed words added for clarity). We read of the "King of kings," of the "Lord of lords," and the "Holy of Holies." We now study the "Song of songs."

I. Intimacy Commenced
(First Love)
Song of Solomon 1:2 – 2:7

Your first experience with the Lord is when the Holy Spirit draws you to Him. What you experienced with Him is termed "salvation," the "new birth," or even "regeneration." Many terms are used to express that first wonderful meeting with the God of heaven through the Lord Jesus Christ. Many consider this to be the ultimate experience. As important as it is, there will be other experiences along the way as you learn to walk with Him. It is an eternal journey that will end with you saved, secure, and resurrected bodily into His glorious presence. When you get there, you should not be "a stranger in paradise." He draws you to follow Him in a continuously closer fellowship until you meet Him face to face in glory. This "drawing" will never cease. For that I am profoundly thankful.

THE LONGING (1:2-3)

Verse 2 says, *"Let Him kiss me with the kisses of His mouth. For Thy love is better than wine."* These are kisses of forgiveness. The prodigal son received this type of forgiving kiss from his father upon his return from wandering. There are all sorts of kisses, you know. Judas gave Jesus the kiss of betrayal. In the New Testament, we are told to greet each other "with a holy kiss." So, the kiss here is an expression of forgiveness, not only once but many times. The Lord forgives you time after time of your sins, mistakes, errors, and shortcomings. We are all prone to these human failings. But He keeps on "kissing" you with the kiss of forgiving love. That is what this is all about. He does not save you and bring you into His family and then abandon you like a baby on a doorstep. He nurtures you, carries you, protects you, and is there for you every moment. That, my friend, is eternal *Agape* love.

When Paul said, "I long to know Him …" he was not speaking of knowing *about* Him, as I pointed out in the introduction. Read with me the full passage in Philippians 3:10 and 11 out of the Amplified Bible: *"[For my determined purpose is] that I may know Him [that I may progressively become more deeply and intimately acquainted with Him, perceiving and recognizing and understanding the wonders of His Person more strongly and more clearly], and that I may in that same way come to know the power outflowing from His resurrection [which it exerts over believers], and that I may so share His sufferings as to be continually transformed [in spirit into His likeness even] to His death, [in the hope] that if possible I may attain to the [spiritual and moral] resurrection [that lifts me] out from among the dead [even while in the body]."*

Please note these facts: There are three words in the Greek language for the word "know." One, *ginosko*, means "to take

I. Intimacy Commenced (1:2 – 2:7)

in knowledge"; another word is *epiginosko*, which means "to know in a fuller, broader and more explicit way." However, in the passage above, the word is *oida*. This means to "fully know." The equivalent in the Hebrew language is *yada*. It means literally "to have intercourse." The word *yada* is used when the Scripture states that Adam "knew" his wife and she conceived a child. The word "know" is an intimate word for bride and bridegroom. This is delicate, I know, and you must not think carnally here. In that relationship there is a strong natural yearning, a "hunger" and "thirst" to *know* each other. So it should be, in the spiritual sense, with the Bridegroom and His bride.

Do you long to *know* Him, to have fellowship with Him, and to be consciously in His presence? Do you have a heart-cry for Him, just for Himself? Do you want Him just for Him and not for something He can do for you? Do you hunger and pant for Him as the deer pants for the stream of water? Psalm 42:1-2: *"As the deer pants for the water brooks, so pants my soul for You, O God. My soul thirsts for God, for the living God. When shall I come and appear before God?"*

How you answer these questions will somewhat indicate to you where you are in your relationship with our Lord. This is the starting point of your spiritual life. Matthew 5:6: *"Blessed are those who hunger and thirst for righteousness, for they shall be filled."* What is that righteousness? It certainly is not your goodness nor bearing. Second Corinthians 5:21 tells us that He (Jesus Christ) is made unto us righteousness. You search for Him for He *is* that righteousness. First Corinthians 1:30: *"But of Him are ye in Christ Jesus, who of God is made unto us wisdom, and RIGHTEOUSNESS and sanctification, and redemption"* (KJV) (emphasis added).

How, you may be thinking, do I find that hunger and thirst for Him? Simply put, ask for it! Spend time seeking His face. Praise Him and become consciously aware of His presence. Seek Him as you would cold water in the mountains if you were dying of thirst. Search for Him in the same manner you would search for foods in a forest where you were starving. There is a quiet desperation here that few folk ever find. Perhaps you will "enter in." I pray that you shall.

Any experience that is legitimate with the Lord will be based on His blood atonement and your intimate knowledge of Him. There will be many *"saved; yet so as by fire"* (1 Corinthians 3:15), for *"if the righteous scarcely be saved, where shall the ungodly and sinner appear?"* (1 Peter 4:18). However, complacency in salvation is dangerous. Churches are filled with "babes" who never go on to "know" the Lord. They get embarrassed when you talk of Him on a one-to-one basis. You may speak of the church, doctrine, or some service to the Lord and have a lively conversation. When you begin to speak of Him on a personal note, however, of His goodness and all His attributes, the other person gets "nervous" and looks around to see if others are listening. Say to others, *"Let Him kiss me with the kisses of His mouth"* and see what happens. This is much too intimate for most folk.

I. Intimacy Commenced (1:2 – 2:7)

This statement was made by the Shulamite maiden to those others around her. She wanted them to know that she longed for Him and to have that intimacy of love. You think this disgraceful? Have you never read Psalm 2:11-12: "Serve the LORD with fear, and rejoice with trembling. KISS THE SON, lest He be angry …" (emphasis added). Here is the ultimate intimacy with the Lord. There is no harshness of duty here; no demands of conscience, but a cry from you for Him to kiss you and a cry from Him for you to kiss Him. Here is reverent and holy worship at its highest.

Note the second phrase of verse two in our text, where she speaks directly to her Bridegroom. *"Thy love is better than wine,"* she cries. She turns from those around her and concentrates on Him alone. Wine, in the Old Testament, is a symbol of joy and fellowship and lifting the spirit of a person. The Israelites served wine to their guests as we serve some popular beverage to our guests. She is saying here that His love is better than all human fellowships and joyousness. Nothing that makes men "happy" and at ease can be compared to the joy that comes from the love of your Lord, the Bridegroom.

(NOTE: From this point forward, I will be referring to YOU as the counterpart of the Shulamite maiden.)

The longing for your Lord is expressed further in the third verse of this marvelous book. You state, *"Thy Name is as ointment poured forth."* His dying for you on the cross was an ointment of love for you. The Name that is above every name is "sweet and soothing and like a melody to the heart. There is a balm in Gilead," and He is that balm, that ointment poured forth. At the cross, you see Him "poured out" for you and His "soul made an offering for sin" (see Isaiah 53:10). You run to that Name when in distress, to that One who is called Savior, Elder Brother, Bridegroom, Master, Wonderful, Counsellor, Prince of peace, the mighty God, the everlasting Father, the King of kings and the Lord of lords!

The last phrase of verse three declares, *"Therefore do the virgins love Thee."* These virgins are the people of God, who have been born again by His grace as expressed in Matthew 25. Why do the saints of God love Him? Because of Who He is! You love Him for one reason only: not in order to get something from Him, but because of Who He is. It is impossible to love "things," such as power or service or doctrine. You may admire and like these and other things, but you can love only a living person.

He is alive! The Seraphim in Isaiah 6 declare Him, *"Holy, holy, holy is the LORD Almighty …"* (NIV). The awesome God is found in your Shepherd-King. He places that love for Himself in you, and you respond with all the other redeemed souls. The word "virgins" in verse three of our text means "hidden *ones.*" Psalm 83:3: *"They have taken crafty counsel against thy people, and consulted against thy hidden ones."* The true children of God are "hidden," and you have to be one to know another "hidden one." The world does not know you, even if you are in the organization of a church. The ones who are not redeemed but members of the local establishment will not know you either. You are "hidden," praise the Lord!

THE DESIRE (1:4a)

"Draw me, we will run after Thee ..." This desire for the Lord has been breathed into you by the Holy Spirit as you have read His Word and prayed. It is not possible to long for Him as a person, unless it is stirred in you by Him. Psalm 37:4 *"Delight thyself also in the Lord ..."* Is it not amazing that the directives, orders, or commands of the Lord are absolutely impossible to do in the flesh?

Think about these commandments: *"Thou shalt love the LORD thy God with all thy heart ..."* or *"... Thou shalt love thy neighbor as thyself"* (Matthew 22:37, 39). Come on! These are impossibles, unless He, by His power, does it in you and for you and through you. No wonder you cry out, *"Draw me ..."* Remember that Jesus said, *"And I, if I be lifted up from the earth, will draw all men unto me"* (John 12:32). You sense His drawing and the effect it will have on you and others.

May I call your attention to the fact that you are continuously undergoing change? Nothing ever remains the same, but God. Malachi 3:6: *"I am the Lord, I change not; therefore ye sons of Jacob are not consumed."* The moment you were born you began to change, and you will continue to do so on through the metamorphosis of the grave. People who do not believe in change, change. You are either getting closer to the Lord or farther away. There is no plateau of sameness.

This begins with a question for you to answer truthfully before the Lord. Is He, to you, ABSOLUTE or ABSTRACT? The word "Absolute" means "actual or real; perfect in itself; unlimited in power; unlimited in purity in Whom nothing can be added." The word "Abstract" means "apart or withdrawn; not representative; imaginative and not realistic." If you feel He is apart from you, He is not really representative of actual life.

There are two revelations here that we need to see. First, we must have a revelation of Him as He is. See Him for Himself, not for what He does for you but for *Who* He is. I cannot stress this point enough because it is the very heart of intimacy. If you are married and really in love with your mate, you do not love that one for what they do but who they are. If you do not feel like that, then you have prostituted your marriage, and it is no more than a civil contract for economic and security reasons. Love the Bridegroom for *Who* He is.

The second part of that revelation is that you need to be drawn to Him, not for what He can do for you, but for His pleasure in you. He does get pleasure from His own. Psalm 149:4: *"For the LORD taketh pleasure in His people: He will beautify the meek with salvation."* We are made for His pleasure. Revelation 4:11 makes it clear that we were made for His pleasure. "Draw me" should be your prayer, as it was the Shulamite lady. Cry out to Him, "Overcome me and my wants and desires. Overcome my pride and my egotism. Overcome my flesh and draw me to Yourself, O beautiful

I. Intimacy Commenced (1:2 – 2:7)

Bridegroom of the church."

The second part of the first phrase in 1:4 is, *"WE will run after Thee …"* (emphasis added). If you are drawn to Him, then it follows that others will be drawn also. No person lives who does not have some influence on someone else. You are not an island. When you see His face and are drawn to Him, others also will seek His face and the intimacy with Him that He desires.

THE INTIMACY (1:4b, c)

"The King hath brought me into His chambers …" These chambers are rooms. They are places of communion and worship and rest. These are the *"heavenly places"* of Ephesians 2:6 where He sits at the right hand of the Father. That portion of Scripture reads, *"And hath raised us up together, and made us sit together in heavenly places in Christ Jesus."* You will find this same beautiful thought in Psalm 91:1: *"He that dwelleth in the secret place of the most High shall abide under the shadow of the Almighty."* Here is a complete abandonment to Him. "Most High" here means "Possessor."

God, we know, owns everything, but He does not possess everything. Even many of His own He does not possess. He has bought them with His blood, but they are not possessed of Him. Speak of demon possession, and we shrink from such a horrible situation. I am not so sure but that we shrink also from the expression of being "God possessed." That in the mind of many would be fanatical. God does draw us to fully abandon ourselves to Him. He is our Bridegroom and our life. As a bride submits to her lover-husband, so should you submit *all* of you—spirit, soul, and body—to your heavenly Bridegroom, Jesus Christ the Lord.

The Lord saved you from sin and continues His salvation in your life. Philippians 1:6: *"He which hath begun a good work in you will perform it until the day of Jesus Christ."*

Note with me the last phrase of the fourth verse in our study: *"... we will be glad and rejoice in Thee, we will remember Thy love more than wine; the upright love Thee."* Some translations show the last phrase as: "They will love Thee uprightly."

You cry out in this moment of intimacy that you and the other virgins will be glad and rejoice "in Him." Satan is a clever foe and one of the ruses he uses is diversion. If he can get you more interested in praise than the One to whom you offer praise, he has diverted your worship to the means rather than to the Person. If you rejoice in the message or the esthetics of the building or in the praise of the people more than concentration on Him, then Satan has accomplished his purpose in keeping the Lord from being the center of your worship.

Intimacy with the Lord demands full attention on Him, not on the means or the method of praising or praying to Him. You are saying that you will remember His love more than the wine of fellowship with other Christians, the "taste" of good times, the "smell" of other companions, the "sight" of the most beautiful edifice of worship, the "hearing" of the greatest songs of adoration, and the "feeling" of the service agenda. You begin to worship Him *"in spirit and in truth."* There are no mixed motives in your love. The purpose is *"... love, which comes from a pure heart and a good conscience and a sincere faith"* (1 Timothy 1:5). Herein is joy! The "joy of the Lord" cannot be taken from you by mere man. Happiness will fade but "joy of the Lord" is in the Lord. It is His joy that you experience. He is always abiding, ever eternal and always *in* you with that wonderful, joyous presence.

THE INNER ROOM (1:5-7)

While in this "room" with your Lord, the proximity of His presence and the overwhelming delight of His love causes you to cry out, *"I am black but comely, O ye daughters of Jerusalem, as the tents of Kedar, as the curtains of Solomon."* You speak this to the other Christians around you. The *"daughters of Jerusalem"* are within the borders of the Kingdom, as typified by the phrase *"heavenly Jerusalem"* in Hebrews 12:22 and *"mother of us all"* in Galatians 4:26. These, however, seem to lack the fervent desire to "know" Him as you do. This Shulamite represents only those of us who long to *"know Him, and the power of His resurrection"* of Philippians 3:10. The *"daughters of Jerusalem"* here are of the same class of "virgins" that had no oil in their lamps when the Bridegroom came. It is suggested here that they represent a lukewarm, compromising, beclouded, or casual Christian, content with "religion," church attendance on a more or less continual basis, and nominal obedience. A good title for these is "barely saved." First Peter 4:18: *"If the righteous scarcely be saved, where shall the ungodly and sinner appear?"* They seem to have no warmth for the Lord, no "bride's passion" for their Savior-King.

I cannot but call your attention to the fact that there are "chambers" where you are. It seems that one must go from room to room, ever closer to the "Holy of Holies" of His presence. I recall from my own experiences that there are degrees of intimacy with Him. Call each of these "experiences" a room or chamber, and you get the idea.

The first thought you have as you are drawn to Him in His "secret place" is that you are not worthy. You see the "blackness" of yourself and your selfishness in every facet of your life that does not flow from Him and His presence.

But, you also see your "comeliness," or beauty, that you have in Him. Your righteousness is of Him in His Son. The Father sees you in His Son, and therefore, you are "beautiful." You see both areas of yourself. The *"tents of Kedar"* mean "dark room" because of the Bedouin tents made of black skins. In this same passage, you speak of the *"curtains of Solomon."* These curtains were made of fine linen and, thus, portray your righteousness in Christ. Revelation 19:8: *"And to her* [the bride of Christ] *was granted that she should be arrayed in fine linen, clean and white: for the fine linen is the righteousness of saints"* (bracketed words added for clarity). Your

I. Intimacy Commenced (1:2 – 2:7)

beauty is in Him. While black with flesh sins, you are beautiful in His righteousness. Hallelujah!

You cry to those other "virgins," the *"daughters of Jerusalem,"* that *"The sun has looked upon me"* in verse six (DT). This is in a tense that denotes an accomplished fact. You are a "burned one." This verbal phrase is in the indicative mood. You cry to them, "Look not on me." Is it not truth that we wish to appear to others to be better than we really are? Our natural failings are an embarrassment to us. The danger here is that the end result would be hypocrisy. We would "put on an act" of being what we really are not for the benefit of others.

"My mother's children were angry with me …" (1:6b). Here again is the wording of Scripture that indicates the heavenly Jerusalem as the mother of the *"daughters of Jerusalem,"* (Galatians 4:26-28). These *"children"* represent those who cling to objective doctrine and denominational status but are without subjective experience with the Lord Himself in a personal way. They are satisfied with their status quo in life. They remain immature in spiritual matters but take a strong stand on all doctrinal issues. They "contend for the faith" by being contentious and unloving with those with whom they disagree. By the way, "faith" does not necessarily mean your peculiar interpretation of some Scripture passages that you have put together as your doctrine of life.

These *"mother's children"* will assume authority over you, if you are not very careful. They will point out that you are "going off the deep end" in your determination to seek the

Lord and find His face. As my friend, Jack Taylor, has so often said, "If I am going off any end, it will be the deep end; you can break your neck going off the shallow end."

You enter that room, that secret place, and have time with your Lord. The result is a marked difference in your life and in your face. The *"mother's children"* will scorn you and privately warn you of the dangers of "going charismatic," words of stigma in the vocabulary of those who are more interested in doctrine than a pursuit of Him personally. Your deep desire is to *know* the Lord, as well as to know *about* Him, and that will bring out bitter feelings and resentments from others.

"... They made me the keeper of the vineyards, but my own vineyard I have not kept" (1:6).

They give you jobs to do, under close supervision, such as teaching a class or serving on a committee. You will be kept busy "doing service" for the Lord so much that you will not have time to care for your own personal vineyard. I have noted this in church after church where I have served. Good people who basically love the Lord are so busy doing "church work" that their own spiritual lives are unkept and, sadly, neglected. What a pity. I have noted, with deep sorrow, many pastors who started out being very intimate with the Lord. Then, the demands on their time from the organized church and the rush of events have slowly taken them away from that time of being alone with the Lord. They, in taking care of the vineyards of others, have neglected their own vineyard and that of their family.

I. Intimacy Commenced (1:2 – 2:7)

I beg you, for God's sake, your own, and that of your family, do not neglect your own "vineyard" at home. I nearly made this mistake a few times in my 60+ years of preaching His Word. I "fed the sheep" by the Word of God, visited the sick and shut-ins, attended committee meetings, and did all the other duties of a busy pastor and evangelist. I spent little time in the Word of God, except to find sermons, and made plans without His guidance, then asked Him to bless those plans I had made. I attended few services to hear other ministers for my own soul. If I went to the Convention, it was to "politic" for a larger church or more revivals. The messages I did hear gave me opportunity to use some of the material in my own sermons. I was shallow, inept, and unhappy.

I awoke to the problem through the concentrated prayers of others and began to spend much time with the Lord. I preached from the overflow of my own vineyard instead of trying to prune the vineyards of others and pumping up enthusiasm for some cause. The more time I spent with Him in personal imtimacy, the more meaning I found in His ministry through me to others. We should be fountains for others to drink of Him, vineyards to bring forth fruit for the hungry, and messengers of personal encounters with our beloved Bridegroom.

Verse seven (1:7) says, *"Tell me, O Thou whom my soul loveth, where Thou feedest, where Thou makest Thy flock to rest at noon: for why should I be as one that turneth aside by the flocks of Thy companions?"*

In this private room with Him, you see the vanity and hopelessness of external service as a religious act. You recognize that the need is not a system of works but an unique walk with Him where He feeds His flock, as a good Shepherd-King. Here is wonderful rest. Here is blessed food. *"Noon"* indicates a time when labor ceases and rest and food are taken. Every child of God must learn to *"turn aside"* from the everyday duties and pressures and spend time with the Lord, that is, if you intend to live long and well for His pleasure and glory.

You are asking Him why you should take time to turn aside and find the flocks of His companions. As you ask this question of your Lord, you seem to be aware that these "companions" are His ministers and "the flocks" are their groups or churches. The structure of the sentence seems to imply that these *"companions"* feel that *"the flocks"* are their own to care for, rather than His people. The words, *"turneth aside"* suggest detraction from the main purpose of your life, which is fellowship with and pleasure to the Lord. The main course of your life is to fellowship with and pleasure your Bridegroom. Seek Him first and all these other things will be added to you. The words *"turneth aside"* could be interpreted as "veil herself." Why should you be one who hides yourself from His feeding to stay with those *"companions"* who do not feed of His love and Word?

I. Intimacy Commenced (1:2 – 2:7)

THE KING SPEAKS (1:8-11)

"If thou know not, O thou fairest among women, go thy way forth by the footsteps of the flock, and feed thy kids by the shepherds' tents (1:8). In this secret place, the room of the Lord, you have seen three things: 1) You are "black" in Adam; there is nothing good in your flesh. 2) You are beautiful in Christ because of His righteousness. 3) You need spiritual food and rest for your spirit and soul, just as much as you need those two things for your body.

Hebrews 4:9-10: *"There remains therefore a rest for the people of God ..."* (NKJV). Your cry to Him is for Him to tell you where *His* flock rests and feeds. Not all "flocks" are of the Lord. There are many churches that are established by man and not by God, although some of the attendants may be Christians. You should seek God's choice for you in attending worship services in a local congregation. Tradition and sentiment *should not* be the ruling factors in this important phase of your life. By the way, *"footsteps"* in this text literally mean "heelprints."

He calls you *"fairest among women"* in verse eight (8). This is because of your capacity to love Him, as small as it is at this time. Your deep desire for Him is the basis for that statement. The Lord is keenly aware of your longing to know Him as He desires to be known. This is the foundation for all communication with the Bridegroom.

The words *"if thou knowest not"* seem to imply that you should have known to love Him first before doing "service" for Him. The *"footsteps of the flock"* speaks of those, like yourself, who have the same urging and desire to seek Him for Himself.

There is only one flock and only One Shepherd. Ezekiel 34:23: *"1 will set up one shepherd over them, and he shall feed them..."* Everyone who has been redeemed belongs to that flock, and the Lord Jesus Christ is the Shepherd. We have been trained, sad to say, to think with a sectarian mind. That should change as you walk with the Lord. The word *"footprints"* or "heelprints" speaks of a vital walk in Him with others in a corporate experience. That corporate experience is vital to you because you are one member of His body, and others are in that body also. You need them to function properly, just as each member of your physical body needs the other parts to function properly. Therefore, to be of a sectarian mind is to hinder His work in you to others. You are a Christian *first*! You should think as His child, not as a member of a particular church or denomination. God is not a Baptist God, a Methodist God, nor an Assembly God. God is God! He will not adapt to our particular mood or mode. He seeks those who will worship Him *"in spirit and in truth,"* regardless of the denomination to which they belong.

The word *"feed"* means to "shepherd." The Shepherd leads His flock where the sweet waters flow and the sustaining bread of life from the Word of God is daily eaten for spiritual energy and joyous life. The Lord is your Shepherd. There is no reason for "want." He knows all about you and

I. Intimacy Commenced (1:2 – 2:7)

what you need every moment of your life. He will supply that need as you are led by Him. He never drives you but *"leads you by still waters."* He always restores your soul areas of will, intellect, and emotions. He never leaves you but is always there for your protection and care. If you should stray, He will leave the ninety and nine and seek for you until He finds you. Remember that your Bridegroom is also your Shepherd and King.

The word *"kids"* indicates lambs, ones less mature, for whom you have responsibility. Your desire for food and rest may surmount your desire for Him, and the result would be a neglect of your responsibilities to others who are less mature than you. You cannot ignore your family and become a hermit. God will not bless this attitude. You love Him through loving those for whom you care, those that have been given to you to care for by His grace. In seeking His face, His personal love for you, His presence, and His fellowship, you must avoid an exclusive attitude toward others. Your seeking His face and resting in Him does not make a monk out of you, and there can be nothing but humility on your part. Intimacy with Christ does not promote pride. You cannot be secluded in your own private little monastery, unapproachable by others and irritated by anyone who might interrupt your "quiet time."

Note that the word *"shepherds"* is a plural word. It speaks of undershepherds. Your position is alongside these men who are called of God. Again, in your pursuit of intimacy with Him, you must remain at the side of the undershepherd, for you are responsible also to him. One of the hardest things to remember, and has become a problem to so many, is that you must be subject to the authority of the one God has placed over you. Humility is a salient feature of the one who is intimate with Christ. You always sense your "smallness." Listen to Paul in Ephesians 3:8: *"... who am LESS than the least of all saints ..."* (emphasis added). In this area, as you seek intimacy with your Lord, you may have conflict with church authority at times. You will pray much and seek His face about these matters. There is a fine line between delegated authority and the command of the Lord to you. There need be no conflict here. Your Lord's word to you is final and irrevocable, but be careful of arrogance as you speak to your shepherd in his authority in the church. Walk with him in love, and do not feel superior to him in your intimate walk with the Lord Jesus.

THE KING CONTINUES TO SPEAK (1:9-11)

"I have compared thee, O my love, to a company of horses in Pharaoh's chariots." The words *"my love"* are better translated "lover friend." *"A company of horses"* is an interesting phrase. Solomon brought his horses from Egypt [1 Kings 10:28-29]. Egypt is symbolic of the world, and you have natural God-given beauty, which the terms *"Pharaoh"* and *"Egypt"* seem to imply. In verse eleven (1:11), we will read of the work of God wrought in you that your intrinsic beauty comes only from Him. However, your attitude of haste makes the Lord speak of the plunging, snorting desire of the highly-

I. Intimacy Commenced (1:2 – 2:7)

bred animals to speed away. It is a beautiful analogy.

Five items signify five areas in your life at this point of your spiritual growth in "knowing" Him:

1) *"A company of horses in Pharaoh's chariots"* means that a good amount of our accomplishments have come from a natural ability.

2) *"Thy cheeks"* implies one's natural poise.

3) *"Braided hair"*—"of jewels" (not in the original text)—is symbolic of the touch of the hands to enhance the natural beauty.

4) *"Thy neck"* signifies a gentleness learned from parents and society, acquired through careful training. In manifestations of "flesh" learned from others lies great danger. Many have a natural "charisma" in preaching or teaching, and they "perform" with affectation learned from others or gained from inside imaginations. Those of us who are in ministry need to learn that we must have His anointing upon us and all that we do if we are to be used of Him in an effective way.

5) *"We will make thee borders of gold with studs of silver"* is the eleventh verse mentioned in the last paragraph. This wonderful verse is filled with great truths for you. Look with me at this work of your Bridegroom in your life. The word *"we"* signifies the Trinity—Father, Son, and Holy Spirit. The Father draws you, the Son saves you, and the Holy Spirit fills you. Yet, there is *one* work in you and for you.

"Borders of gold" symbolizes the divine character of God-made personality. The word *"borders"* mean "wreath." It takes

time and intricate care to beat and form precious gold into a lace pattern as a border around an object. It is very delicate work. It takes time for the Lord to work His heavenly character into you. This work takes the place of your braided hair of natural beauty and charisma in the ministry God has for you.

Finally, the *"studs of silver"* refer to the basic and foundational redemption by the cross of Calvary where our Savior bled and died for us. He is continuing the work of the cross in your life. You are continually "being saved" in order that others might come to Him and find the redemption He bought for them. You should meditate on the fact that the Godhead of Father, Son, and Holy Spirit is interested in you and your being like Jesus. You are special, and you are important to Him who bought you with His blood.

YOU SPEAK AGAIN (1:12-14)

"While the King sitteth at His table, my spikenard sendeth forth the smell thereof. A bundle of myrrh is my well-beloved unto me; He shall lie all night betwist my breasts. My beloved is unto me as a cluster of camphire in the vineyards of Engedi."

Solomon's table has deep and significant meaning pointing to the Lord Jesus Christ. If you will take time to pick up your Bible and read 1 Kings 4:22-23 and 1 Kings 10:5, you will see the extent of provision by Solomon for his family, servants, and guests. This speaks of the provision of the Lord for you. All these "things" are yours if you seek Him first

I. Intimacy Commenced (1:2 – 2:7)

instead of the "things."

"While the King sitteth at His table" represents His fellowship with you around the provisions He gives you. They are His for you to enjoy with Him, and, for these, He receives from you praise and adoration. Walk by the sea and enjoy the blue sky, the green water, the white sand, and the cool breeze. Those are His "things" for your enjoyment because He loves you. He is with you in the enjoyment of these things.

"My spikenard sendeth forth the smell thereof." When you enjoy what the Lord enjoys, then praise is spontaneous. There is a smell or "sweet odor" of praise lifted to Him with Whom you dine. Praise always corresponds to fellowship with Him.

The word *"well-beloved"* in verse thirteen (1:13) should read "Bridegroom-lover." *"Myrrh"* signifies suffering love for you. When Jesus was on the cross, He was offered wine mingled with myrrh. This is an exceedingly bitter concoction. Also, Nicodemus brought myrrh with which to anoint His body for burial. Myrrh was used as a part of the embalming fluid. It was an ingredient of the holy anointing oil and was one of the gifts of the wise men who came to worship Jesus at His birth. Suffering love is a rare commodity. Not many will give their life for their friends, much less for their enemies. Jesus did so, and the world was His enemy then as it is now.

The next phrase, *"he shall lie all night betwixt my breasts,"* is such an important statement with such spiritual content that I make this separate paragraph to explain what it means. The un-spiritual person would immediately think of this in a carnal way. I want you to see this in its pure and beautiful context. *"Night"* speaks of separation. The Lord is in heaven at the right hand of the Father and separated from you in His physical person. Yet, He lies all night between your breasts. In Scripture, the two breasts of a woman represent *faith* and *love*. First Thessalonians 5:8: *"But let us, who are of the day, be sober, putting on the breastplate of FAITH and LOVE ..."* (emphasis added). Here you are saying that during the night of His long physical absence from the earth, you will hold Him to your heart with *faith* and *love*. Our God is known as Jehovah-Jireh, which literally means, the "twin-breasted One." Galatians 5:6 tells us that "faith worketh by love," and they are twin attributes for the saint of God. These 12th and 13th verses convey intimate communion with the Bridegroom-King. It is, of course, in the spirit. The inner room of the heart, or spirit, is private, personal, and full of praise for Him whom your soul loveth.

The fourteenth (1:14) verse conveys the subject of being adorned and clothed with the Lord Jesus Christ. *"Camphire"* is henna flowers. Jewish maidens used them for adornment upon their bodies. *"Engedi"* is a place of vineyards. This is where David fled to hide from Saul. Flowers do not normally grow there. This represents the fact that you confess Christ before men, talk of Him instead of mere doctrine or organization, and thus make Christ as a sweet bouquet of "camphire" to be seen and smelled of others. Camphire, or henna flowers, has a delightful odor. Note with me, in this conjunction, 2 Corinthians 2:15-16 (AMP): *"For we are the sweet fragrance of Christ [which exhales] unto God [discernable alike] among those who are being saved and among those who are perishing: To the latter it is an aroma [wafted] from death to death [a fatal odor, the smell of doom]; to the former it is an aroma from from life to life [a vital fragrance, living and fresh]."* You emit or give off a spiritual odor, if you please, when you dwell with Him in His secret place and all, lost or saved, "smell" you. Once in Houston, Texas, I accompanied an attorney friend of mine with two detectives to apprehend a criminal. We entered a nightclub and were seated at a table. Within three minutes, one of the detectives turned to me and said, "Reverend, you better get out of here and go to the car. These people know you do not belong here." There was a "smell" about me that those lost people recognized unconsciously.

THE KING PRAISES (1:15)

"Behold, thou art fair, my love; behold, thou art fair; thou hast doves' eyes." The eyes of a dove are truly beautiful. I have seen people with the type of eyes that look like they could melt and run down on their cheeks. They are soft and beautiful, indeed. This should be the eyes of every Christian, full of compassion, love, and grace. They represent spiritual insight or perception, which makes you attractive to the Lord. The eyes of a person, someone has said, are the windows of the soul. Let me look into your eyes directly for a few minutes,

and I'll read your spirit. Jesus said in Matthew 6:22: *"The light of the body is the eye: if therefore thine eye be single. thy whole body shall be full of light."* I have met individuals who had "hard" eyes. They looked like hardened steel, with no love or compassion, but filled with suspicion and malice.

As you sit in His presence and commune with Him, your *"eyes"* of understanding things as He sees them become very acute. The Lord never made judgements based on natural seeing or hearing. He judges with "righteous judgement" (see Isaiah 11:3-4). We, to be like Him, must be filled with Him to do the same thing. As you spend time with Him in that intimacy of love, you grow more and more like Him in attitude and meeting life day after day. Read with me the Scripture mentioned above: *"... and He shall not judge after the sight of His eyes, neither reprove after the hearing of His ears: but with righteousness shall He judge the poor, and reprove with equity for the meek of the earth ..."* You begin to do as He does. With righteousness, He ever makes decisions, and you do the same. "With equity," you would *"... reprove, rebuke, exhort with all longsuffering and doctrine"* (2 Timothy 4:2). You must learn that this is God's way of living in the midst of society.

YOUR RESPONSE (1:16 - 2:1)

"Behold, thou art fair, my beloved, yea, pleasant: also our bed is green. The beams of our house are cedar, and our rafters of fir. I am the rose of Sharon, and the lily of the

I. Intimacy Commenced (1:2 – 2:7)

valleys." You cry out to Him, after He speaks of your eyes, because He is enjoyable and such a blessing and pleasure to you. His compliment enhances the love you feel for Him. You tell Him that He is *"pleasant"* or pleasing to you. I would to God all Christians could bask in His pleasantness. There is such joy and pleasure just being in His presence and involved in such a personal, intimate manner with the Maker of the universe. He is pleasant, kind, and gracious, a joy for you and a pleasure for Him to have communion with each other.

"Our bed is green." A bed is for resting the body. This passage speaks of the "rest" of Hebrews 4:9: *"There remaineth therefore a rest to the people of God."* Reference here should also be made to Psalm 23:2: *"He maketh me to lie down in green pastures …"* Green pastures are beds for sheep to rest, watched over by the shepherd. The green bed is a resting place where our Great Shepherd, Jehovah-Rohi, watches over us. He furnishes us with spiritual food, water of the Word, and rest in Him. What a wonderful Shepherd is ours!

"The beams of our house are cedar, and our rafters of fir," verse seventeen (1:17). In the temple built by Solomon, the woodwork was cedar and fir (cypress). Cedar is symbolic of the humanity of Christ. The "death tree" of the East was cypress. This represents His dying for you so that now you "rest" in His perfect manhood and His perfect atonement for you. Timbers of cedar and cypress were worthy construction materials in Solomon's temple. They represented the Lord Jesus Christ in the building and speak of His worthiness. You,

also, are a *"temple of the Holy Spirit,"* and God dwells in that place represented by cedar walls and cypress floors—His Son's humanity and substitutionary death. Here is where you rest because it is where God is pleased to dwell.

YOU CONTINUE TO SPEAK (2:1)

"I am the rose of Sharon, and the lily of the valleys." Most of our lives we have been taught that this verse describes our Lord. There is nothing wrong with that because He is most assuredly the essence of a gorgeous rose and a beautiful lily. However, to be true to the Word of God, I must point out here a few facts that will change our way of thinking on this matter. The rose is a very common flower that grows amid millions of other roses on the plain of Sharon in Judea. Jesus is not common, as this rose and as we are. Secondly, the lily is the narcissus and grows in the hidden valleys of the plain. In this passage, you are saying, "I am an ordinary person among ordinary people, but I am loved and cared for by my Bridegroom-King. I am just another 'rose' on the plain of life or another 'lily' hidden in the remote valleys of this world, unheard of and mostly unseen. But You, precious Lord, care for me and see me as an individual 'flower.' Flowers you love in this life. Therefore, I desire to emit the sweet fragrance of the lily and the rose so that you may be pleased with the essence of my life."

I. Intimacy Commenced (1:2 – 2:7)

YOUR KING SPEAKS (2:2)

"As the lily among thorns, so is my love among the daughters." He is saying that you are indeed a "lily," but a lily among thorns. You are placed in moral contrast to the unsaved world. Thorns speak of Adam's fall and the natural life of those who have not yet surrendered to the Master of Life, Jesus Christ. Thorns grow of themselves, as do weeds, and need not be tended because of the curse on the ground brought about by the fall (Genesis 3:18). Lilies and roses must be cared for by someone, or the thorns and weeds will crowd them out. This portion of Scripture tells you that God *never ever* uses anything of man's fallen nature. He uses that which only proceeds from Him. You are a new creation, and latent talents in you were placed there before your birth through your DNA, and by His "cultivation," they will be used to please Him and bring glory to His Name.

All of God's attributes flow from intimacy with Him. You desire to be loved? Find His place of intimacy! You crave power? It flows only from intimacy with Him. You want answer to your prayers? In the aura of intimacy with Him come answers to your prayers. You seek healing, or direction for your life, or truth about Scripture? Intimacy is the answer! Intimacy is the answer to your every need. Intimacy is not sought in order to get something from Him. Intimacy is for the sake of pleasing Him and adoring Him for Himself. There can be no hidden agendas or wheedling or whining in intimacy. It is pure love for Him in Spirit and in pure truth.

That is the intimacy that He desires!

The words *"my love"* in our text are deep with meaning. You are different! There is a hint here that you will suffer from the "daughters," saved as they are, because you are "going on." There may be loneliness and misunderstanding awaiting you because you are intimate with Him. There may be jealousy and fault-finding in the days ahead. What do you do in the intimate walk with Him when these things come upon you? Here is the answer!

YOU PRAISE HIM! (2:3-6)

"As the apple tree among the trees of the wood, so is my beloved among the sons. I sat down under His shadow with great delight, and His fruit was sweet to my taste." The apple tree is the citron tree, with beautiful foliage that does not fall in the winter. The fruit looks like a pomegranate but tastes like a tangerine.

You see Him different and unique among all men. He came into the world as a man, but He was both God and man. He was preeminent over all the sons of Adam. There are none to compare to Him.

You rest under His shadow with great delight. Read Psalm 91:1 again and be blessed with the words, *"He that dwelleth in the secret place of the most High shall abide under the shadow of the Almighty."*

The *"fruit"* of His presence and love is sweet to the hungry soul. This is your testimony to others when they look askance

I. Intimacy Commenced (1:2 – 2:7)

at you through baleful eyes. You minister to others. Herein is such an important point! We should minister to the Lord first, and then we will be able and capable to minister Him to others. If you do not do the first, there will be no anointing for the second. Others will say, *"I am of Paul; and I of Apollos,"* etc. When you speak of Him and His intimacy and His delight, you will be told, "I am a Baptist, I am a Catholic, I am a Pentecost," etc. But you say, "That is fine, but I love Him first who loved me first." Your devotion is more personal than a denomination, an organization, or doctrine, or even proving a point. You are in love with a person, not with a method or tenet of belief.

Note the progress you have made and be encouraged. In chapter 1, verse 4, you are running after Him; in the 12th through the 14th verses of the same chapter, you are sitting at His table; in the 16th and 17th verses, you are resting in Him; and, in this second chapter, 3rd verse, you are basking in His presence and enjoying Him with great delight. Sometimes we get so involved that we do not realize just how the Lord "leads His dear children along." Praise God for His attention every moment of every day.

"He brought me to the banqueting house, and His banner over me was love." In this fourth verse, you discover more joy and gladness than ever known before. The term *"banqueting house"* means "house of wine." The King brings you into this place. In chapter 1, verse 4, you were brought into the inner room for revelation. Here, you are brought into the banqueting

house for the joy of His presence. *"His banner over me was love"* demands recognition. "Jehovah-Nissi" means that your Bridegroom is your flag of identification in war. He is the ruling motivation of your life. Each nation has a flag, and people of that nation salute their flag, fight under it, and pledge allegiance to it. Well and good! But you, besides having allegiance to a flag and a nation, have a greater allegiance to the God of the Bible, Jehovah God, Owner and Ruler of all nations. He is your allegiance, and He is your love. His flag flies over your life, and it is known by the love shown in you. The Lord's banner over your camp is the banner of love.

Verse five (2:5) says, *"Stay me with flagons, comfort me with apples: for I am sick of love."* Flagons are grape cakes, and apples are citrons, as noted before. These are delicious foods for the hungry heart. Hebrew words here are in the plural form. You are saying, "Refresh me, for I am exhausted with joy and pleasure." Heavenly experiences tire the human body. In my intimacy with the Lord, I have found that there are times when a personal encounter with Him in the spirit has left me totally exhausted in the mental and physical part of my makeup. As I said, these words, "flagons" and "apples," are used here in plural form. You have more than one encounter with Him, more than one experience with the Shepherd of your soul, and more than one time when He feeds you with the "bread of heaven." No wonder you feel exhausted. But He knows what He is doing with you. He is forming Himself into your life, and your physical body has a

I. Intimacy Commenced (1:2 – 2:7)

hard time keeping up with the beautiful spiritual life you have found in Him.

Verse 6 states, *"His left hand is under my head, and His right hand doth embrace me."* Here again is a picture of Psalm 91:1. His left hand under your head indicates His support of your mental capacities. You are to have the mind of Christ. Philippians 2:5: *"Let this mind be in you, which was also in Christ Jesus."* You let His mind, His thinking, His ability to pleasure His Father become yours by being intimate with Him.

His right hand holds you in His arms of protection. Picture yourself as a child, held in His arms, and His shadow protects you from both the heat of the sun and the storms that rage. There is a two-fold picture here. One, the Father holds you safely in His embrace. Two, as the Bridegroom, He holds you tenderly in His arms of love. Either picture tells us of His care for us and His love manifested.

A WARNING (2:7)

"I charge you, O ye daughters of Jerusalem, by the roes, and by the hinds of the field, that ye stir not up, nor awake my love, till He please." The word *"my"* is not in the original text. The warning here is to "meddlers" with your intimacy. The "daughters of Jerusalem," in this instance, are those fond of ecstatic experiences. They should not meddle with your emotions. If one is prone to interfere with what God is doing in another person, they need to be warned of the danger. *"Touch not my anointed"* is applicable here. Let all keep

silence before His work in each of us. Unless you are very sure that God is sending you to "give them a word," then please do not do so. It is very dangerous, and many a person has been deeply hurt by "a word" from someone who has watched and made a judgement by the seeing of the eyes and the hearing of the ears.

The Lord is the one who awakens love in a person. He is the One who has full and complete control of this area of your life. One Sunday, I was in a church service where I was being "torn" over the devastating illness of my wife. I could not help but weep in desperate need of solace from God. The pastor and one other came to stand by my side, but they uttered no words. That was such a comfort to me. Others of the leadership of this great church knew of the struggle but were wise to let the Lord do His work in me. I praise God for them all.

II. Intimacy Conflicted
(Faltering Love)
Song of Solomon 2:8 – 3:5

In order to fully understand the meaning of "Intimacy Conflicted," one must understand the human design. Later on in this book, I will be referring to the Holy of Holies and how you are "composed" as a human. Suffice it to say now that you *are* a spirit, you *possess* a soul, and you *live in* a body. Therefore, salvation is triune, as are you.

Your **spirit** has been saved (past tense) from the **penalty** of sin; your **soul** is being saved (present tense) from the **power** of sin; and, at His coming, your **body** will be saved (future tense) from the very **presence** of sin. You will be delivered completely in Christ at that moment of resurrection. Paul was used of God to state in 1 Thessalonians 5:23 that he prayed for you that *"… your whole spirit and soul and body be preserved blameless unto the coming of our Lord Jesus Christ."* So understand your triune design and know that, at this present time, He is "saving your **soul**, with its will, intellect, and emotions."

THE CALL FOR SURRENDER OF "SELF" TO HIM (2:8-15)

"The voice of my beloved! behold, he cometh leaping upon the mountains, skipping upon the hills. My beloved is like a roe or a young hart: behold, he standeth behind our wall, he looketh forth at the windows, shewing himself through the lattice. My beloved spake, and said unto me, Rise up, my love, my fair one, and come away. For, lo, the winter is past, the rain is over and gone; the flowers appear on the earth; the time of the singing of birds is come, and the voice of the turtle is heard in our land; the fig tree putteth forth her green figs, and the vines with the tender grape give a good smell. Arise, my love, my fair one, and come away. O my dove, that art in the clefts of the rock, in the secret places of the stairs, let me see thy countenance, let me hear thy voice; for sweet is thy voice, and thy countenance is comely. Take us the foxes, the little foxes, that spoil the vines: for our vines have tender grapes."

You are keenly delighted by the voice of your Bridegroom. But, as of this time, you are not really submitted to Him in *full* surrender. We will note this as we continue. To regard the Lord as a roe or hart (deer) has an obvious meaning. If you study Psalm 22, which we know as the "Messianic Psalm," you will find the title is "Upon Aijeleth Shahor." This means "According to the Hind of the Morning." Most Bible students agree that this points to the Lord's resurrection. Morning is the beginning of the day and the beginning of new life. The spiritual life always begins, not with crucifixion and death, but with resurrection. One must enter into his Lord's death and crucifixion, but if there is no resurrection experience, then there is no life. If Jesus had just died on the cross and never been resurrected, He would have been a martyr and not a Savior. You, too, must go on through the process and find that "resurrection life" for yourself. He will guide you into it.

There are four things here that we need to think about:

1) The Power of the Resurrection in your Life.

Mountains and hills in the Word of God refer either to nations or authorities or, in this instance, difficulties and hindrances. As you hear your beloved's voice and see Him coming to you, you realize that He has your problems, hindrances, and difficulties under His feet. There is nothing thrown at you by Satan that will hinder His coming to you. He is the Risen Lord! He is full of resurrection power. He has triumphed over *all* problems, difficulties, hindrances, and authorities. Because of Him, you are victorious, and He will deliver you "out of all your troubles" (Psalm 34:6). He is your mighty Bridegroom!

The ninth (2:9) verse states, *"My beloved is like a roe or a young hart: behold, He standeth behind our wall, He looketh forth at the windows, shewing Himself through the lattice."* Although His voice is dear and He walks with you to leap over the problems, there is yet a wall between you. He looks in the windows and shows Himself through the lattice that separates you. "What is that wall or lattice?" you ask. It is the self-life.

Between you spirit and your soul is the think curtain of **self**. Just as there was a curtain between the Holy of Holies and the Holy Place in the Tabernacle, so there is a veil, a curtain, between your spirit where the Holy Spirit dwells, and your soul where *you* are in charge. "Self' must be torn asunder from top to bottom, when you can then say, as did your Savior, *"Not my will, but Thine, be done"* (Luke 22:42). The veil between your spirit, where He abides, and your soul area could also be called "self interest." The soul needs to be "filled with the Holy Spirit," so He can use your intellect and emotions to bring glory to His Name. Your spirit has experienced resurrection from death. Now, the same must occur in your soul life. Paul said in Philippians 3, *"... that I may know* [oida] *Him and the power of His resurrection ..."* while yet in the body *(soma)*. Thus, the spirit, soul, and body, in that exact order, become a temple of the Holy Spirit of God. First Corinthians 6:19-20: *"What? Know ye not that your body is the temple of the Holy Spirit which is in you, which ye have of God, and ye are not your own? For ye are bought with a price: therefore, glorify God in your body, and in your spirit, which are God's."* Is it not amazing that your soul is not mentioned here? Why? Because your soul is where your will abides, together with your intellect and emotions. God will never, never overstep your will. He said in one place, *"And ye WILL not come to me, that ye might have life"* (John 5:40, emphasis added). We are made in His likeness and therefore have a will as no other creature on earth has. The soul is "self" territory.

That territory has to be surrendered to Him. We are rebels and we must surrender. We need daily deliverance. This is an on-going matter and it takes resurrection power to overcome the self-life.

2) There is the Provision of the Resurrection Life.

"My beloved spake, and said unto me, Rise up, my love, my fair one, and come away. For, lo, the winter is past, the rain is over and gone; the flowers appear on the earth; the time of the singing of birds is come, and the voice of the turtle [dove] *is heard in our land; the fig tree putteth forth her green figs, and the vines with the tender grape give a good smell. Arise, my love, my fair one, and come away."* (2:10-13).

Here is the **provision** of resurrection. Come out of your self-pleasing, self-gaining, and self-emphasis life. *"The winter is past"* speaks of a cheerless time, which is a time of testing. It is over! Philippians 3:13: *"Forgetting those things which are behind…"* The winter rain is over and gone. Birds and flowers speak of spring time, new life, and resurrection joy. Here, there are songs, adornment of beauty, and praise to God. The turtle dove is cooing his soft and beautiful lament to his mate. The fig tree is bringing forth its fruit. The vines are in blossom. This is a description of you as you come out of your self-life and get absorbed in His life in you. This is resurrection time; abundant life, free from the selfish restraints of the soul; and, here is expression of the power of the resurrected life in your Bridegroom, Jesus Christ of Nazareth.

3) Heed the Call of the Cross.

In verse 14, we read where you continue to speak of what He says to you (verse 10), and it is a beautiful thought. He says: *"O my dove, thou art in the clefts of the rock ..."* A better translation is: "you are in the Rock that was cleft." *"... in the secret places of the stairs, let me see thy countenance, let me hear thy voice; for sweet is thy voice, and thy countenance is comely."* Your Bridegroom is referring to Himself as The Rock that was pierced on the cross; where the spear was thrust into His side; where blood and water came forth; and, where you are hidden! As God opened the side of Adam and took a rib to form Eve as his bride, so has God opened the side of His Son to give Him His bride, the church. Herein you find a subjective experience, and herein is your cry for Him. Listen! The face and the voice of the Lord are always seen and heard in conjunction with the Atonement. Therefore, we live the life of our Lord experientially based on being made *"... conformable unto His death"* (Philippians 3:10).

You are in the *"secret places of the stairs."* I studied and prayed over this phrase for a long time to see His meaning in its translation. I believe the Lord is showing us here that we are to grow in the love and knowledge of Him from plateau to plateau. We have a standing in Him before the Father, but we need spiritual and moral growth if we are to please our Bridegroom. You can become more and more of what you already are in Christ.

When you climb a stair you find "risers." These are the

portions of the stair that cause you to step up. I compare these "risers" to tests of our faith. You move along on a plain or flat surface of life, as shown by the flat part of the stair (the tread). Of note here is that the verb form of "tread" is often used as "treading water"—simply staying afloat; there is no forward motion. When you come to the "riser," you must step up or stay where you are, or worse yet, go back down. You surmount the "riser" with the energy of faith. You step up to a higher plane of life because you exercised faith. From one plane to another, from one plateau to another you move higher and higher. It is by His faith and love that this is accomplished. Also, the higher you climb, the farther you can have vision of the world and the needs of people. These tests of faith are shown by the secret places of the stairs of life.

"*... let Me see thy countenance, let Me hear thy voice; for sweet is thy voice, and thy countenance is comely.*" The Master is saying that "in the cross" your face is sweet to Him and your voice lovely to His ears. His cry to you is for you to cast off all semblance of self for Him.

4) We see His cry for Removal of all Hindrances.

In chapter 2, verse 15, we read, "*Take us the foxes, the little foxes, that spoil the vines: for our vines have tender grapes.*" The little foxes are our enemies. Damage is done by big foxes, but little foxes "spoil" the vine to the extent that no fruit is produced. It is not the big sins but the little habits of life that ruin your fruit. Most of us are careful not to commit the more heinous sins, such as murder, adultery, or thievery. Preach all you want, pastor, on those subjects, but there are "little" habits that ruin our testimony and keep us from being all we should be in Him. In Ecclesiastes 10:1, we read, *"Dead flies cause the ointment of the apothecary to send forth a stinking savour: so doth a little folly him that is in reputation for wisdom and honour."* A little foolish jesting at an inappropriate time outweighs wisdom and honor from someone known to be wise and honorable. Personal habits detract from your attitude of living in Him. These, and, especially, doing the work of the Lord slothfully are all "little foxes." Small matters should be taken to the Lord immediately. Instead of defending our lack of attention to these matters, we should make haste to take them to the Lord for Him to forgive and control. The little foxes of self can certainly hinder the Lord's work in you and through you. We need to *"take us the foxes"* and, with the power of the resurrected Christ, get them out of our lives. This will be a continuous work all the days of our existence on this earth. That should not deter us, for He is quite able to help us in our daily walk to overcome the little foxes of bad habits that detract from Him.

FAILURE AND RESTORATION (2:16 – 3:4)

"My beloved is mine, and I am His" (2:16). All at once, you are aware of the fact that the Lord Jesus Christ lives in you and that He loves you deeply and dearly. You are conscious of His relationship, and it is wonderful. But, as yet,

He is not the focus of your full attention. As yet, you have not responded to His call in chapter 2, verse 10 to "*come away.*" You still persist in being the center. Note what you say and how you say it: *"HE IS MINE, and I am His."* You feel that *you* possess *Him*, and you are proud of that fact, so you hug Him to your bosom like a child with a new toy. *"He is mine ..."* Then you note that *"... He feedeth among the lilies,"* or that He is evident among others who love Him as you do. Psalm 45 is a song of loves or "lilies." Read this passage and be blessed because it portrays the King and His bride, and His victory with us into eternity. Hallelujah!

Psalm 45 (NKJV)

1 My heart is overflowing with a good theme; I recite my composition concerning the King; my tongue *is* the pen of a ready writer.

2 You are fairer than the sons of men; grace is poured upon Your lips; therefore God has blessed You forever.

3 Gird Your sword upon *Your* thigh, O Mighty One, with Your glory and Your majesty.

4 And in Your majesty ride prosperously because of truth, humility, *and* righteousness; and Your right hand shall teach You awesome things.

5 Your arrows are sharp in the heart of the King's enemies; the peoples fall under You.

6 Your throne, O God, *is* forever and ever; a scepter of righteousness *is* the scepter of Your kingdom.
7 You love righteousness and hate wickedness; therefore God, Your God, has anointed You with the oil of gladness more than Your companions.
8 All Your garments *are scented* with myrrh and aloes *and* cassia, out of the ivory palaces, by which they have made You glad.
9 Kings' daughters *are* among Your honorable women; at Your right hand stands the queen in gold from Ophir.

10 Listen, O daughter, consider and incline your ear; forget your own people also, and your father's house;
11 So the King will greatly desire your beauty; because He *is* your Lord, worship Him.
12 And the daughter of Tyre *will* come with a gift; the rich among the people will seek your favor.

13 The royal daughter *is* all glorious within *the* palace; her clothing *is* woven with gold.
14 She shall be brought to the King in robes of many colors; the virgins, her companions who follow her, shall be brought to You.
15 With gladness and rejoicing they shall be brought; they

shall enter the King's palace.

16 Instead of Your fathers shall be Your sons, whom You shall make princes in all the earth.
17 I will make Your name to be remembered in all generations; therefore the people shall praise You forever and ever.

"Until the day break, and the shadows flee away, turn, my beloved, and be Thou like a roe or young hart upon the mountains of Bether" (2:17). The word "Bether" means "separation." It is also called the "mountain of spices" in chapter eight. In this Scripture, you admit there are "shadows," or "little foxes," in your life. You realize with Paul (Philippians 3:13-14): "I have not yet attained, but I press on to the high mark." Here, you are telling the Lord that when the shadows, the little habits, are gone, then you will present yourself. One of the great failures in the Christian life is holding on to a habit and trying to "help" the Lord with our flesh. "I will clean up my life, and then I will present myself to Him." You do not have the ability to clean up your life. He alone has that authority and power to make you clean. The flesh cannot help the flesh. You cannot lift yourself by your own bootstraps. It is His salvation, and He must have your permission to continue "saving" you by His complete control of your life.

He must have the right to pleasure Himself with you, since He bought you by His blood on the cross of Calvary.

So you cry, "... *turn, my beloved* ..." Here are two things upon which to meditate: One, you have fallen behind in following Him; and two, you are insisting on doing things your way instead of His way. There is a lack of ongoing faith because of your insistence that "self" be satisfied. You cry to Him, "Come back to me! Turn, and be like a speedy young deer and come back." You should be saying, "I will follow You in faith. I will go with You at Your pace, not mine. I will follow closely." He has not abandoned you. He is Jehovah-Shammah and, therefore, said He would never leave you nor forsake you.

Instead, in your emotions, you "sense" a separation. This is a pitfall set up by Satan. You must learn that you cannot follow the Lord based on emotions. Walking with Him does not depend upon your present emotional state. You must stay with Him in the circumstances He has arranged for you. The word "circumstance" means you take your "stance" in the center of the circle of events. Let come what may, "... having done all to stand, stand." You must also be careful about introspection. Looking inside of yourself to see how you "feel" and how you measure up with others is a very dangerous game. When the Holy Spirit points out something to you, then you know about yourself. But self can never measure self and come out approved by Him. Only the Holy Spirit has the authority to measure you, since you belong to the Lord, bought by His blood, and He lives in your spirit.

II. Intimacy Conflicted (2:8 – 3:5)

"By night on my bed I sought Him whom my soul loveth: I sought Him, but I found Him not" (3:1). The word "night" here is in the plural. Separations based upon your emotional state are nights of agony for you. The very essence of being separated from Him draws you to Him. When He is not speaking to you, His very silence is speaking to you. But herein lies a question. Are you really seeking Him or are you seeking the emotional satisfaction you have when in His presence? His absence draws you, and His absence spurs you to seek Him. You will never, never be satisfied again without His presence.

"I will rise now, and go about the city in the streets, and in the broad ways I will seek Him whom my soul loveth: I sought Him, but I found Him not" (3:2). Like the prodigal in Luke 15:18, you arise and go out to find Him. You exerted no real effort to find Him while seeking Him "on your bed," but waited for Him to come to you.

Here, we note three steps for the Christian: The first step is knowing *(oida)* the Lord of the cross for salvation from sin; the second step is knowing Him as the resurrected Lord in His indwelling reality; and the third step is abiding in Him in a constant, hour by hour, moment by moment, leading of the Holy Spirit. In this order, there will be no separation from Him in space, place, time, or senses. God disturbs your bed (note that the bed is *your* bed) as the mother eagle stirs up her nest to compel the young eaglet to fly. You are beginning to move out now from *your* rest to *His* rest. You are beginning to seek Him for Himself and not for yourself.

You have been involved in books, doctrines, commentaries, studies about Him and in meetings of sundry types. Now you are seeking Him for *Him*. This is the very thing He has desired of you. The church employs ways of having fellowship with each other. It is good; all the above is good. But this is better! Now you seek His face and His presence for Himself. You do not cover up your need of Him, the desire to please Him, nor do you save face by pretending all is well. He has placed a hunger in your soul to know Him in a more personal way than ever before. *"Blessed are they which hunger and thirst after righteousness* [the Righteous One]: *for they shall be filled"* (Matthew 5:6. Bracketed words added for clarity). Hunger and thirst must be instilled in you by the Lord because the flesh will not, nor can not, do it. The "old man" does not want to seek Him. All sorts of doubts of your salvation or experiences with Him really bring questions to your mind. The enemy assails you with fiery darts to confuse you and keep you from that personal intimacy you desire. Satan never stops fighting this one area of a Christian's life. If he can succeed here, then he has you trapped in mediocrity and compromise the remainder of your life on this earth.

"The watchmen that go about the city found me: to whom I said, Saw ye Him whom my soul loveth?" (3:3). The watchmen are those who are called to watch for the souls of men, the ministers of God. Hebrews 13:17: *"Obey them that have the rule over you, and submit yourselves: for they watch for your*

souls, as they that must give account, that they may do it with joy, and not with grief: for that is unprofitable for you." The watchmen can do no more than point the way or give the right instructions. This verse does not tell us what, if anything, was said to the Shulamite girl. These watchmen were possibly not that closely in contact with the Shepherd-King. It is very sad to say that, many times, ministers of all kinds are so busy in the affairs of church that they do not take time with Him.

Usually, when doubts arise in our hearts, we turn to others whom we deem spiritual enough to give us answers. At times, this is good, but there are times when no one can give you the answers but the Lord Himself. Only He has the answers to your needs.

"It was but a little that I passed from them, but I found Him whom my soul loveth: I held Him, and would not let Him go, until I had brought Him into my mother's house, and into the chamber of her that conceived me" (3:4). Although you are yet imperfect, the Lord is pleased to be found of you because of your honest search for Him. He brings you through measured waters as described in Ezekiel 47. But, even now, you desire to be in control. You hold Him and will not let Him go. Friend, He cannot be "held" or controlled, nor was this meant to be. He is the director of your life, and you are His to lead, direct, and control. When you seek Him in this spiritual way, He moves at His pleasure, not yours. Soulish seeking of the Lord will produce selfish interests, even in His presence. In the description of the measured waters of Ezekiel

47, mentioned above, you will find a "flowing." You move with that flow into a deeper and deeper Spirit-led life until you are "swimming" in the waters of His will and His grace.

The Lord deals with each one of us in our individual capacities. In this place, you do not discern the difference between spirit-seeking and soul-seeking. So, the Lord meets you on your level. He does not run away but teaches you where you are in the growth pattern of "knowing" Him. *"My mother's house"* represents the system of teaching of grace and love you have always known. You would bring Him into your particular denominational system or "religion" and cause Him to fit in your organizational pattern. You know your "mother's house," and even "into the chamber" where you were "born again" would you bring Him. Concentrate on this fact that the Lord Jesus Christ does not adhere to any manmade system. He is not a Catholic God, a Baptist God, or any other denominational God. He is GOD! He works within all these systems, but He is Possessor, Ruler, and Maker of all. He cannot be circumscribed by men's systems of worship.

YOU WARN THE "DAUGHTERS" (3:5)

"I charge you, O ye daughters of Jerusalem, by the roes and by the hinds of the field, that ye stir not up, nor awake my love, till He please" (3:5) You warn others not to interfere with your spiritual development. He alone will deal with you. Too many people in the church are determined to direct young Christians in the manner they think best. With advice

and teachings of some sort or other, they try to guide the newly saved. It is so fine to teach and direct these "infants" in the Lord, but be reminded that *you* are not the teacher. The Holy Spirit is the only one who can teach them without error. He can and will use the teacher or minister, but the teaching must come from Him. Look at 1 John 2:27: *"But the anointing which ye have received of Him abideth in you, and you need not that any man teach you: but as the same anointing teacheth you of all things, and is truth, and is no lie, and even as it hath taught you, ye shall abide in Him."* The anointing, or the Holy Spirit, abides in you and is your teacher. He uses ministers and others who are vessels of His, but the teaching comes from Him *if it is truth*. Give glory to no man for his teaching ability. His ability comes from the anointing of the Lord, and your reception of what is taught comes also from the anointing of the Lord. In this manner, He gets all the glory.

III. Intimacy Communicated
(Flourishing Love)
Song of Solomon 3:6 – 5:1

A NEW CREATION

By His grace and love, you are beginning to see what He seeks in you. His desire is to create in you the image of Himself. You are "resting" in Him, but is He "resting" in you by the Holy Spirit? The Lord's ways always originate in His grace and love. No matter how many failures you may experience, He continues to draw you to Himself. However, you must not dwell on experiences.

Many seek the experience rather than the Lord. I made this mistake in my journey through my desert. I sought the experience of the infilling of the Holy Spirit for a long time and found nothing. He showed me that I was seeking an experience instead of seeking Him for Himself. When I came to Him simply because I love Him, then and only then did I experience what I deem to call "His Fullness."

In this section, you will find yourself more intimately and deeply involved with Him than ever before. You are climbing the stairs of knowledge of Him and His working in your life. The passages in this section will enlighten you only if you have followed the sequence of events and surrendered to Him as you have come along.

"Who is this that cometh out of the wiilderness like pillars of smoke, perfumed with myrrh and frankincense, with all powders of the merchant?" (3:6). Your companions, the "daughters of Jerusalem," are probably the ones who ask this question. At any rate, whoever it is, they are amazed at what is going on in your life. The picture here is of a procession of mighty men bearing a litter on which your Shepherd, King, and Bridegroom sits with you. You are coming up from the wilderness, a place of wanderings. You have wandered in several directions in your seeking to know Him on an intimate basis. Now you are coming to an end of your wanderings and wonderings. You are entering real rest. You are entering *His rest*. Here, resting in Him, you are beginning to desire to so live that the Heavenly Father, with all His attributes, may be expressed through you. In this manner, He gets the glory, and that is what you desire.

Complete union is revealed in this passage of Scripture. Herein is a description of your journey with Him. The phrase, *"like pillars of smoke,"* indicates a new faithfulness brought about by His intimate power in you. There is strength and dependability evidenced in you. Revelation 3:12: *"Him that overcometh will I make a pillar in the temple of my God ..."* Pillars are the portion of a building that hold the edifice together and keep the upper part in tact. The meaning here is that the strength and ability of the Holy Spirit is being manifested in you, so that you are visibly stable.

III. Intimacy Communicated (3:6 – 5:1)

"Myrrh" in this verse is an indication of your subjective sense of the value of His sufferings for you. You are becoming more aware of the high cost He paid to bring you to Him. You are beginning to bear the sweet odor, or fragrance, of Christ as evidenced in Philippians 3:10: *"That I may know him, and the power of his resurrection, and the fellowship of his sufferings, being made conformable unto his death."* You now have the power of a depth of love that gives forth the fragrance of Christ. Read 2 Corinthians 2:15-16 again on this thought:

> *For we are to God the fragrance of Christ among those who are being saved and among those who are perishing. To the one we are the aroma of death leading to death, and to the other the aroma of life leading to life. And who is sufficient for these things?* (NKJV)

"Frankincense" refers to the risen and triumphant life of Christ, with special reference to His being a living High Priest. Revelation 8:3 speaks of an angel with much incense: *"... that he should offer it WITH THE PRAYERS OF ALL SAINTS upon the golden altar which was before the throne"* (emphasis added). Your prayers go up mixed with the incense, a part of which is frankincense, to the Lord as a sweet savor to our God who sits upon the throne. He lived and died to live again eternally. So you must be identified with Him in His resurrection power. This is why myrrh is mentioned first, referring to His death, and frankincense is mentioned second, referring

to His resurrection.

"With all the powders of the merchant" indicates the price paid by Him, and now the price paid by you for that identification. You must pay the price of complete surrender and absolute obedience. That is what He did to save you, and you must enter into those attributes of the Lord. Identification is a necessity for you to continue with your Master. There will be mountains and valleys; deserts and jungles; and, there will be all sorts of experiences with men, angels, demons, and your own imagination. Through it all, cost what it may, your ever-present Lord will never fail you nor leave you.

"Behold his bed, which is Solomon's; threescore valiant men are about it, of the valiant of Israel. They all hold swords, being expert in war: every man hath his sword upon his thigh because of fear in the night" (3:7-8). Around the litter, or bed, on which you are riding with the Bridegroom, there are guards. This speaks of your triumph over your enemies. He rests, and you rest in and with Him. You are now so identified together with Him that His enemies are your enemies. The *threescore* (60) *valiant men* around you are angels, called the "heavenly host." These are the ministering spirits to the heirs of salvation mentioned in Hebrews 1:14.

I would to God that you knew of your divine right to have angelic protection. Briefly, there are three bands of angels who serve you and surround you as you rest in Him. One is the guardian angel or angels; the second is the group of ministering angels that came to Jesus in the wilderness; and, the third group is the band of warring angels that are loosed to fight the demons of hell. You should take time to make a study of this angelic band. It would encourage and bless you as you go on with your Bridegroom.

"King Solomon made himself a chariot of the wood of Lebanon. He made the pillars thereof of silver, the bottom thereof of gold, the covering of it purple, the midst thereof being paved with love, for the daughters of Jerusalem" (3:9-10). This is the second reply to the one who spoke in verse six (6). The chariot was a covered litter carried on the shoulders of men. It was carried in the same manner as the Ark of the Covenant, with staves resting on the shoulders of the bearers. Here is wisdom: the movements of the Lord are carried by those who are identified with Him in His death, burial, and resurrection. The litter was made of wood, which represents human nature. Cedar from Lebanon is superior wood from a high place and indicates our Lord's superior manhood. He was taller than most of His peers, noble, stately, masculine, and perfect in body, soul, and spirit. The silver pillars denote the grace of redemption.

This is a picture of our Lord Jesus Christ brought into human history to conquer death and bring life to whomsoever would accept Him as Lord and Savior. This passage stresses the work of the cross in your life of identification with Him. The floor of the litter was made from gold and, thus, shows that the ground or basis of movement is always in the divine character of our God.

The curtains that cover this vehicle are purple. This is the color of royalty. Jesus is King! The government is upon His shoulders, and He will reign until all enemies have bowed beneath His feet, including the last enemy, death. Can you imagine the thrill that should be yours in the spirit as you are carried on the same litter with the King of kings and Lord of lords? You reign with Him! You are made a king and a priest because of Him! This is who you are, my friend.

> Revelation 1:4-6 (NKJV): "... *Grace to you and peace from Him who is and who was and who is to come, and from the seven Spirits who are before His throne, and from Jesus Christ, the faithful witness, the firstborn from the dead, and the ruler over the kings of the earth, To Him who loved us and washed us from our sins in His own blood, and has made us KINGS AND PRIESTS to His God and Father, to Him be glory and dominion forever and ever. Amen."* (Emphasis added.)

The inside of the litter is paved with love. Love is all around you; agape love of the Lord never ceases or changes. He *is* Love, praise God! All of this is a vehicle for His movements *in* you and *for* you. The Lord finds His place of "going forth" in the natural affection and the love you now have for Him.

YOUR BRIDEGROOM SPEAKS (4:1-5)

In this passage, the Lord speaks of your beauty to Him. He gives a seven-fold description of your spirit by using the physical beauty of the Shulamite maid in the language of love used in that day and time.

"Behold, thou art fair, my love; behold, thou hast dove's eyes within thy locks ..." (4:1a). The eyes speak of perfection. Others can see Him in your eyes. I have already spoken of dove's eyes and how one can really be made to think of Jesus when looking in the eyes of one who spends much time with Him. There are people who have looked at me, and I believed they were reading my soul and knew everything about me there was to know. There is a depth to those eyes that is hard to describe.

Here is danger! Be careful as you look on others with compassion. The phrase *"within thy locks"* really is interpreted "behind the veil." Your eyes can be shrouded for safety's sake. Un-spiritual people will not understand what you perceive. Be careful that you do not express in an indiscriminate way the things God has revealed to you. The more you love Him and have an intimate walk with Him, the more "dove-like" will become your eyes. A carnal man or woman will see you look at them with the eyes of compassion and immediately prostitute that gaze to mean something sexual and sinful. *"Within thy locks"* is a safe place for your eyes of love to be. In other words, be exceedingly careful as you notice others, lest they misread your look of compassion.

"*... thy hair is as a flock of goats that appear from mount Gilead*" (4:1b). Here, the hair speaks of special consecration and obedience, as in the case of a Nazarite (Numbers 6). The hair depicts strength and dedication, as in the story of Samson. Hair is a covering and shows subjection to Christ, or it means rebellion against Him. Many today wear long hair as a "sign" of rebellion. It is the very opposite of what long hair was designed to depict in the Bible.

You are a holy offering to the Lord. Here is where your hungry spirit is fed, and He is blessed by you. Micah 7:14: *"Feed thy people with thy rod, the flock of thine heritage, which dwell solitarily in the wood, in the midst of Carmel: let them feed in Bashan and Gilead, as in the days of old."* You are well fed by Him and ready for His purpose for you at any given moment.

"Thy teeth are like a flock of sheep that are even shorn, which came up from the washing; whereof every one bear twins, and none is barren among them" (4:2). The teeth speaks of the ability to appropriate and use that which the Lord gives to you. There is a sufficiency of spiritual food for you or anyone else who would walk with Him in an intimate manner. However, not all have the ability, it seems, to receive that food. Babies cannot masticate what adults eat. They do not have the teeth for it.

A *"flock of sheep"* suggests all of your ability (as a full set of natural teeth is there to eat and masticate what He supplies). Herein lies a truth that many have missed. It has been taught that one must study much to be able to understand the Word of God. Understanding the Word of God does not come from much study but from the enlightenment that comes from the Holy Spirit. Much study should be done and is profitable, but the understanding of what God means in His Word comes from intimacy with Him, rather than an intellectual acumen. As I said before, striving to know what God is saying can produce an inferiority complex in those who have not had the benefit of study under learned men. The least Christian has the ability to understand, by the Holy Spirit, the basics of the Word of God. *"Study to show thyself approved"* means to give diligent thought how you can pleasure Him and be approved of Him. Study is one way, but there are also many other ways.

You have the ability to understand and be taught by Him if you will seek Him for Himself, notwithstanding what others may say to you. What He says and what He means in any given passage of Scripture is the determining factor of teaching. To teach Scripture as doctrine with "proof texts" is fine, I suppose. But anyone can match up specific Scriptures and prove about anything that they desire to prove. That is not the way to interpret the Word. Let Him speak to your heart, and then follow the Holy Spirit in the interpretation, using all the tools of scholarship you desire. Study the Greek and Hebrew languages, peruse commentaries, and read after scholars. Please do that. But, the final truth of the Word comes from Him.

By the way, "wool" in Scripture indicates the carnal life and natural zeal. The priests were forbidden to wear wool garments (Ezekiel 44:17). They wore linen clothes as a symbol of purity. Here, you are "shorn" of your natural ability, zeal, or persistence, and your natural, religious desires.

"... which come up from the washing; whereof every one bear twins ..." (4:2b). This phrase tells us of good and orderly ability, by the Holy Spirit, to receive revelations from the Lord. Your natural teeth are in pairs, well balanced in your mouth, for the necessary mastication of food to prepare that food for digestion. The Lord will bring you to a balance in interpretation of Scriptures. So many insist on their view of the Word of God and are not balanced in their presentation of the Word. They harp on one doctrine, or play one string, all the time and are unbalanced in interpretation. It is like chewing your food with only half of your teeth. You can get indigestion from food not fully prepared by mastication. Unbalanced Bible teaching is also dangerous because it brings forth division and all sorts of problems for the church. In Isaiah 30:18, we are told that the Lord is a God of judgment (or method).

One must "rightly divide the Word of Truth" if one is to be truthful. One danger in setting all your mental abilities on a doctrine is that you will miss what God is saying. Doctrine is not God. God is God, and He has the ultimate meaning of all Scripture.

"Thy lips are like a thread of scarlet, and thy speech is

comely: thy temples are like a piece of pomegranate within thy locks" (4:3). *"Lips"* means "expression." Your lips are the vehicle for expressing your spirit. A *"thread of scarlet"* indicates two truths: redemption and authority. Jesus was the Word and came to redeem us by shedding His blood on Calvary. A word is not a word until it is spoken or revealed; otherwise, it is a thought. Words coming from your lips bear the authority of your person. You speak what He is saying in your spirit. You speak life, not death; blessing, not cursing; truth, not lies. Remember that *"death and life are in the power of the tongue"* Proverbs 18:1. The Lord desires to speak through your lips the life that is in Christ Jesus, our Lord. Be admonished that Jesus spoke the will of the Father (John 5:30). You and I should do the same.

"Temples" or "cheeks" represent the beauty of emotions controlled by Him (4:3b). Facial expressions reveal the attitude of the person. If you are happy, angry, bewildered, intense, excited, or any other expression of soul feelings, it will be shown by the expression on your face. A *"piece of pomegranate"* denotes something open and exposed to the view of all who look. In the Bible, *"pomegranate"* points to fullness of life because of its many sweet, juicy, and red seeds. I repeat for emphasis, your face reveals your spirit. May it reveal the sweetness and love of your gracious and wonderful Bridegroom.

All of this is seen by Him and the few saints who walk in the same pattern of life seeking His face. However, this attribute is unseen by the world and many of the "daughters of Jerusalem."

"Thy neck is like the tower of David builded for an armoury, whereon there hang a thousand bucklers, all shields of mighty men" (4:4). The *"neck"* represents your will. You have heard of people calling others "stiff-necked." This means that proud, unrelenting will of man. Isaiah 3:16-17a describes this attitude, *"Moreover, the Lord saith, Because the daughters of Zion are haughty, and walk with stretched forth necks and wanton eyes, walking and mincing* [tripping nicely] *as they go, and making a tinkling with their feet: Therefore the Lord will smite ..."* (bracketed words added for clarity). Proverbs 6:17-19 lists seven things the Lord hates. One of these is "a proud look." This is in regard to the will of man that disregards God and what pleasures Him. You are not described as these, but He says your neck is "like a tower," which suggests steadfastness, hope, encouragement, and a bearing of looking up toward Him. It could be illustrated by the face of a young bride as she looks up into the face of her beloved new husband. The woman in Luke 13:11-16 was "bent down" or "bowed together." All she saw was the earth in front of her. This is the picture of so many Christians in this life. Satan causes them to be "bowed down" with cares and sorrows and the self-life as he did this pitiful woman. But Jesus set her free, and her neck became straight "like a tower." If you *must* have your own will above what He wants, then the best description of you is that you are "bowed down." However, in this passage He sees you established in Him with a *"neck like the tower of*

III. Intimacy Communicated (3:6 – 5:1)

David builded for an armoury." Here is a fact of faith that you are now confident in Him, and you know He will guide you, love you, protect you, and bless you for His pleasure, as well as for yours.

So, you have been brought into complete obedience, a person after God's own heart, as was David. One would think that after David's problem with Bathsheba and her husband, God would never say that David was a man after His own heart. But God said in Acts 13:22, *"And when He had removed him* [Saul], *He raised up unto them David to be their king; to whom also He gave their testimony, and said, I have found David the son of Jesse, a man after mine own heart, which shall fulfill all my will"* (bracketed words added for clarity). God said this because David humbled Himself and repented. Therefore, God removed his sin from him as far as the east is from the west and remembered it against him no more. You, too, can be a person after God's own heart. He is no respecter of persons. Repent of every idea, work, or anything you can think of that does not please or pleasure Him. Set your affection on things above, not on things of the earth. Seek His face, and do that each and every early morning. Neither you or anyone else has the right to go back after your repentance and accuse you of sinful acts. When God forgave and forgot your sin, no man has the right to place himself above God and accuse you. This is why judging is such a horrible sin on the part of the one who judges. Forget the past, and permit no one to bring up the past, with its mistakes, to your memory. You now walk with Him. You have today and all the tomorrows for His glory. Forget the past and go on in humility and love.

The battle of life is around the will. God made you to have a choice. That is why He made you in His image. No other creature has a will and a vocabulary like a human. This is what makes man so different from all other forms of life. This is the reason that evolution is so much nonsense. Do as Jesus did and say, *"Not my will but Thine be done."*

"Bucklers" and *"shields"* are instruments of protection and war. A buckler (Heb. *Romah*) is a sword. You have the *"sword of the Spirit, which is the word of God,"* and you have the *"shield of faith,"* as recorded in Ephesians 6. A *"thousand bucklers"* means that you have the entire Word of God as a Sword against the enemy. Every passage of Scripture is a "buckler" for you to use against Satan. With the "shield of faith" to stop his fiery darts, and in the strength of the Lord, you have already won the victory. Gird on the armor, take the shield, and grasp the sword in your hand for battle. The *"mighty men,"* which are the angels of God, surround you, and the Lord Himself is your rear guard. You have nothing to fear. So march on, O child of God, in victory!

"Thy two breasts are like two young roes that are twins, that feed among the lilies" (4:5). *"Breasts"* symbolize the seat of your life. As stated in earlier pages, the breasts of a woman represent *love* and *faith*. The Scriptures tell us that "faith worketh by love" (Galatians 5:6). The words in this passage

about the breasts tell us they are *"like two young roes that are twins."* Young roes are naturally shy and very alert and nimble. They are hidden by their mother from the eyes of predators. Such faith and love are not for public attention.

The original text states, *"A pair of young deer born of the same mother."* There is no imbalance here. You are not great in faith and small in love, or great in love and small in faith. These are twin attributes. Galatians 5:6: *"For in Christ Jesus neither circumcision availeth any thing, nor uncircumcision; but FAITH WHICH WORKETH BY LOVE"* (emphasis added). Your faith "works" by your love. You cannot have more faith than love.

Another passage that emphasizes this point is found in 1 Timothy 1:14: *"And the grace of our Lord was exceeding abundant with FAITH AND LOVE which is in Christ Jesus"* (emphasis added). The idea is again shown to us in Philemon 5: *"Hearing of thy LOVE AND FAITH, which thou hast toward the Lord Jesus, and toward all saints"* (emphasis added).

Another point to consider is that faith and love may both be little or large, great or small (as a woman's breasts). But they are twins and equal. The Lord is not speaking of the size of your faith and love but stressing the fact that they should be balanced and equal. Also, consider that you are to put on the breastplate of righteousness (Ephesians 6:14). The breastplate of righteousness is love and faith. Without love and faith, there is no righteousness. First Corinthians 13:2: *"… and though I have all faith, so that I could remove mountains, and have not charity* [love in action], *I am nothing"* (bracketed works added for clarity). As stated before, these attributes are seen and feed *"among the lilies,"* who are the children of God with whom you associate on a daily basis.

NOW YOU SPEAK, represented by the Maiden (4:6)

"Until the day break, and the shadows flee away, I will get me to the mountain of myrrh, and to the hill of frankincense." In chapter three (3), you spoke of your union with the Lord. In chapter four (4), the Lord found satisfaction with your progress. Now, having come through some wilderness experiences, there is a difference in your speech. If you will note, your words are fewer, and you give more attention to Him and what He says. You remain quiet before His praise, and you do not sense the swelling of pride over His praise, your accomplishments, or how He sees you. You are very aware of the fact that all this has come about because of Him, and His work in drawing you to Himself.

This is a beautiful fact that we need to note. So many, upon rising in accomplishments of one sort or another, permit pride to ruin their walk with the Lord. They talk more of themselves and what they are doing than speaking of Him and His work.

You have a deeper sense of your weakness, and you cry out—Heed this!—you cry out for a deeper work of the cross in your life!

"Until the day break and the shadows flee away ..." is

your way of saying, "Until resurrection morning and the shadows of this life are gone." In other words, you are determined that while He is bodily in heaven seated at the right hand of His Father, you *will* have purpose in your life. You *will* live and not just exist as a mortal. You are determined to live unto Him, for Him and His pleasure. There are still "shadows" in your life, and the perfect day has not yet dawned. The more light you have from Him, the more obvious is the blackness in your own life. The nearer you walk with Him in intimacy hour by hour and day by day, the more you are aware of your own imperfections. You feel your immaturity. The more praise that comes from His lips, the more humble you become. When you state, *"I will get me to the mountain of myrrh and the hill of frankincense,"* you realize that you have not "arrived" as yet. You need to know more of the myrrh and the frankincense of His resurrection life.

The only solution for now until He comes for you, is death to the self-life and praise to God for His resurrected life in you. I heard an old, old song many years ago, a part of which said, "Oh, deeper, Lord, I pray, and higher every day: And wiser blessed Lord, in Thy precious, Holy Word." Amen!

HIS CALL TO LIVE IN THE HEAVENLIES

In this area of "flourishing love," growing deeper, and rising higher, the King speaks to you of that upward movement. You realize that, according to the first and second chapters of Ephesians, He is seated in the heavenlies and that you are already seated with Him in your spirit. Again, as I have said before, He desires you to experience, in fact, what He has declared you to be in Him.

THE SHEPHERD-KING SPEAKS (4:7-15)

"Thou art all fair, my love; there is no spot in thee." (4:7). He told you in the first verse of this chapter that "you are fair." Now He says that "you are *all* fair" to Him. Your negatives and your blemishes are being removed. He sees the end result of His working in you by the Holy Spirit. He will present you "faultless before the throne of glory." What a salvation! Your spirit has been saved, and that is called *Justification*; your soul is being saved day by day, and that is called *Sanctification*; and, your body will be resurrected. Your whole spirit, soul, and body will be presented "faultless before the presence of His glory" (Jude 1:24), and that is called *Glorification*. That salvation has been bought by our Lord Jesus Christ; to Him is all the glory and praise. I do not often deliberately repeat myself, but these are areas that bear repetition.

"Come with me from Lebanon, my spouse, with me from Lebanon: look from the top of Amana, from the top of Shenir and Hermon, from the lions' dens, from the mountains of the leopards" (4:8). The Lord never lowers His standards, nor does He ever surrender His purpose for you. He never changes His call to you, nor does He ever stop drawing you

to Himself. You are being called to higher and more noble places. *"Come with Me,"* He says.

This verse means that He is asking you to come and view life from the top of the mountains of difficulty where the "lions" and "leopards" crouch. Here are "mountain-top" experiences. We tend to define mountain-top experiences as emotional highs in public or private worship. These are wonderful times, it is true, but the real mountain-top experience is when you are on top of your difficulties with Christ through faith.

This verse means that He is asking you to come and view life from the top of the mountains of difficulty. With every mountain of difficulty, there He is, awaiting you to protect and free you. Here is *"Amana,"* which means "confirmation of truth." His Word is truth, and, on top of that difficult place, it will become obvious that He keeps His promise. Only on *top* of the mountain, not *under* the circumstance, do you find Him and His deliverance.

The mountain called *"Shenir"* means a "flexible armor." We have noted this before, but on *top* of these mountains, you are clothed with Him as in Ephesians six (6). This armor is found only when you walk with Him on *top* of the difficulty.

The mountain called *"Hermon"* denotes the destruction of Satan and the final victory of the Lord Jesus Christ. Jesus came to destroy the works of the devil, and He is busy doing it at this moment in you. Many are the problems and difficulties, it is true, but He is on *top* of them all. These are the mountains where the presence and the warfare of the enemy become very real. Here are the "lion's dens" and the "leopard's lairs" of enemy assaults. Satan goes about, the Word tells us, like a *"roaring lion seeking whom he may devour"* (1 Peter 5:8).

"Come with me," Jesus says, to the top of these mountains where the real enemy works; where life really is, in the school and market place; and where you hear the "roar" and "screaming" of the enemy. In Christ Jesus, your Bridegroom, you have the armor, the strength, and the victory to overcome, and God will get the glory. If you do not know the experience of Ephesians one (1) and two (2), it is doubtful you will experience the victory of Ephesians six (6). Read all these chapters for your edification, and *"Come"* with Him to place your feet on top of your problems, for He has already won the victory for you.

Mountain tops with Him is imperative. God forbid you seek to walk on top of your mountains of difficulty without Him. Those mountains can become Victory mountains, mountains of Divine Truth, mountains with protective armor, and mountains of great victory over all the wiles and attacks of the enemy. Here is where you "pull down strongholds" and "cast down imaginations"! Come to the *top* with Him, and see the vision. Take your position in Him. He is above and not beneath; He is Victor and not loser; He is to be trusted and loved. Learn the art of intimacy with your Bridegroom. You will find deliverance and victory in Him.

"Thou hast ravished my heart, my sister, my spouse; thou

III. Intimacy Communicated (3:6 – 5:1)

hast ravished my heart with one of thine eyes, with one chain of thy neck" (4:9). For the first time, the King addresses you in the double role that you have with Him. You are called His *"sister,"* made so by His death on the cross and His resurrection from the dead unto life. He is your Brother, your Elder Brother, because of the Father. You are in the family of God.

You also carry the title *"spouse,"* or wife. Note this verse very carefully. You are called *"sister"* first, and then you are called *"wife."* Husbands, if you and your wife are both Christians, then realize that she is your sister in the Lord first, and then she is your beloved wife. I never saw this until my wife of over fifty years was afflicted with Alzheimer's disease. I did not know at the outset how to handle the problem. I tried unsuccessfully to meet the situation in the emotional and intellectual realms, but I could not find satisfaction there. My reasoning did no good, and my emotions helped far less. So I did as I should have done. I went to the Lord in prayer, and He led me, as He always does, to a passage of Scripture. (His Word has the answer to all problems.) This Scripture (4:9) gave me the answer. I saw her as my sister first and then as my wife, and I was comforted to meet the conditions imposed upon me. Jesus is the Elder Brother for each one of us, and then He is our precious Bridegroom. These are symbols of our relationship with Him.

Your desire for Him, brought about by His constant love evidenced toward you, is now identified with His desires for you. You are now giving pleasure to Him. That is what

Christianity is all about, you know. *"Sister"* means kinship, and *"spouse"* means relationship. Hebrews 2:11a: *"For both he that santifieth and they who are sanctified are all of one." "There is one Lord, one faith, one baptism,"* (Ephesians 4:5) one family, and only one Bridegroom and one bride. Praise the Lord!

"Thou hast ravished my heart …" (4:9a). His heart that was broken in Gethsemane and pierced on Calvary is "ravished" by your spiritual perception. That word means "to be enclosed with." You love Him for Himself. He is "enclosed" with you and your love. A stranger cannot read the eye of love, but He is no stranger. He is your Brother-Bridegroom. He reads your love, and His heart is "enclosed with you," or "transported with love." The primitive root of this word indicates that His heart is filled with your love, and He is therefore filled with pleasure and joy.

"… with one chain of thy neck" (4:9b) indicates the ornament of grace found in the stance of your neck, as we have noted before. Proverbs 1:9: *"For they shall be an ornament of grace unto thy head, and chains about thy neck."* This concerns the wisdom and teaching of godly parents. He knows He can lead you deeper into His wisdom, grace, and love. Some will not go with Him deeper every day, but He notes your will to do so, and that is a pleasure to Him.

"How fair is thy love, my sister, my spouse! how much better is thy love than wine! and the smell of thine ointments than all spices!" (4:10). This speaks of the drawing power of

our Lord. We call it the "convicting power of the Holy Spirit." God, the Father, chose to draw men to Himself through the Lord Jesus Christ. The Lord said, "*And I, if I be lifted up from the earth, will draw all men unto me*" (John 12:32). To draw men, Jesus, as God's Son, had to shed His blood on the cross of Calvary as the "*Lamb slain from the foundation of the world*" (Revelation 13:8). God chose this act of love to draw us to Himself. Through the death and resurrection of our Lord, you were invited to come into the family of God; to love Him and become a member of His royal entourage; and, by doing so, express His love on this earth to all men. Christ is the center to whom all response to the love of God must move. There is no other way to receive God's love nor to approach the Father except through the Lord Jesus Christ. Jesus said, "*That all men should honor the Son, even as they honor the Father. He that honoureth not the Son honoureth not the Father which bath sent Him*" (John 5:23). He also said in John 14:6: "*I am the way, the truth, and the life: no man cometh unto the Father, but by me.*"

This love for the Father and the Son matures as you go on with Him. You love Him more today than you did yesterday and less today than you will tomorrow. You are getting to the place where you are going to "*Set your affection on things above, not on things on the earth*" (Colossians 3:2). You have upon your spirit the fragrance of His ointments. This is the same Holy Spirit that came upon Mary to impregnate her with the Holy Seed called Jesus Christ of Nazareth; the same

Holy Spirit that directed Him all His days on the earth; the same Holy Spirit that came upon Him in the form of a dove at His baptism by the hands of John the Baptist; the same Holy Spirit that drove Him into the wilderness to be tempted of Satan; the same Holy Spirit that raised Him from the dead and seated Him at the right hand of the Father. That same Holy Spirit, I say, that anointed and led Jesus Christ now anoints you. The human mind cannot contain such thoughts. Only the heart (spirit) can receive these blessings from God. You are in fellowship with Him to such an extent that Psalm 133:2-3 is evident in your life. That Psalm states, *"It is like the precious ointment upon the head, that ran down upon the beard, even Aaron's beard: that went down to the skirts of his garments; as the dew of Hermon, and as the dew that descended upon the mountains of Zion: for there the* LORD *commanded the blessing, even life for evermore."*

The fragrance mentioned here is invisible and is discerned only by the sense of spiritual perception. This perception, or discernment, is a spiritual quality, a life fashioned by the Spirit of the living God. This is the anointing that brings out the following words:

"Thy lips, O my spouse, drop as the honeycomb ..." (4:11a). It takes time and work to manufacture, accumulate, and assimilate honey. Study the busy bee, and see the manufacture of this sweet substance. It takes time also for you to learn to say sweet and edifying words instead of idle and negative statements. Your praise of Him and your words of life come

from your lips for all to hear, especially the Lord, who hears every word that comes from your mouth and knows your thoughts before they are spoken. You speak life and not death. Look at Proverbs 18:20-21: *"A mans belly shall be satisfied with the fruit of his mouth; and with the increase of his lips shall he be filled. Death and life are in the power of the tongue: and they that love it shall eat the the fruit thereof."* You will eat the fruit of your own mouth whether it speaks life or death. The Lord is blessed when you speak life and blessing.

"... honey and milk are under thy tongue ..." (4:11b). Honey represents immediate strength, and milk builds bones and sinews. All of these analogies speak of the work of the Holy Spirit in your entire life cycle. While most of us tend to rattle on about anything and everything, making "small" talk, we must realize that we will give account for every idle or unprofitable word that we speak. Here, the Lord is saying that your mouth, tongue, and lips speak that which is strengthening and building Christian character in others while blessing and pleasuring Him whom you love.

"... and the smell of thy garments is like the smell of Lebanon" (4:11c). Garments, in Scripture, speak of attitudes, actions, and behavior. Garments are seen by everyone. Your behavior is seen connected with the mountain-top experiences with Him. Many speak of mountain-top experiences, as we noted before. We mentioned the fact that the experiences during difficult days can be the mountain-top times with the Lord. The clean scent of the cedar on top of Lebanon

wafts to Him from your trust, faithfulness, and attitude. Your "garments" smell good.

"A garden enclosed is my sister, my spouse; a spring shut up, a fountain sealed" (4:12). This passage is pungent with meaning. Note the word *"garden"* is in the singular, meaning *one* garden. God started with just one garden, called Eden. He will end with one garden, called heaven. A garden is generally for the production of food that has sustenance, beauty, and pleasure to the eater. There are all sorts of trees in this garden. Trees for building, trees for fruit, and ornamental trees for the esthetic pleasure of the Owner and His guests. He now calls you a *"garden,"* and you are *His* garden. You are for His pleasure and are in a spiritual condition to delight, satisfy, and pleasure your Bridegroom. You do not now live or exist for yourself, but for Him and His pleasure. You have a high calling. You are a *"garden enclosed,"* a *"spring shut up,"* and a *"fountain sealed."* This is not a public garden where just anyone may come in. You are endowed with all the necessary attributes for His use. You are for Him and for His guests that He may invite to partake of your life. You *must* be careful that you do not expose your heart to just anyone or everyone. Numbers 19:15: *"And every open vessel which hath no covering bound upon it, is unclean."* Clean vessels are kept covered. You do not, as a garden, a spring, or a fountain of the water of Life, throw yourself open to all that enter your pathway of life. You are enclosed, shut up, and sealed to all except the Bridegroom and those He brings to you as His

III. Intimacy Communicated (3:6 – 5:1)

guests to be fed of your fruit and favor. This will keep you from "casting your pearls before swine."

Note this verse very carefully. Your Bridegroom is giving you a warning. He said in Matthew 7:6: *"Give not that which is holy unto the dogs, neither cast ye your pearls before swine, lest they trample them under their feet, and turn again and rend you."* How many times have earnest and zealous Christians told of their experiences with the Lord before unbelieving, sneering and doubting people. In return, those saints received wounds from their sharp tongues as they *rend* you for your sacred meeting with your Lord. Only those, I repeat, that the Lord shares His "garden" with should know of your intimate experiences with your Bridegroom.

However, I must reiterate with emphasis that you are for *His* pleasure first. This is the reason He wants you, as His garden, "enclosed," "shut up," and "sealed." You are for HIS enjoyment. He "eats" of the fruits He has planted there. Think on this! When Jesus died on the cross of Calvary, it was to satisfy His Father's desire first before it was to save you. Both came to pass at the same instant, of course, but He died in obedience to His Father's will and to satisfy the blood covenant He had made at the very beginning, before the foundation of the world. As He satisfied His Father, so He saved us. His obedience to His Father was the salvation provided for mankind. Romans 5:19: *"For as by one man's disobedience many were made sinners, so by the obedience of one shall many be made righteous."* The point is that *always*

He is first to be loved, satisfied, and pleasured because He is God who sustains and keeps you.

"Thy plants are an orchard of pomegranates, with pleasant fruits; camphire, with spikenard, spikenard and saffron; calamus and cinnamon, with all trees of frankincense; myrrh and aloes, with all the chief spices" (4:13-14). Note the garden as your Bridegroom continues to speak. *Plants* here mean "sprouts." He is saying that you are full of power. You now know the resurrection power that conquers death, and you now live in that resurrection power and life, even while yet in the physical body. Your vitality is likened to an orchard of pomegranates. You are a garden full of an abundance of fruit for Him and His guests. The trees and plants mentioned here emphasize color and fragrance. Your fruits of grace are glorious. Second Corinthians 9:8 says: *"And God is able to make all grace abound toward you; that ye, always having all sufficiency in all things, may abound to every good work."* You will note the different plants and trees and resins mentioned here. Spikenard was an aromatic oil used for anointing; camphire was a cream-colored flowering plant with a sweet aroma; saffron gives forth a wonderful odor; calamus denotes reeds that are usable for quills, etc. Cinnamon, frankincense, and myrrh are all gum resins used in the holy anointing oil by the priests, and aloes is the perfumed oil from the tree of the same name. All of this denotes in you a bold and heady perfume in the nostrils of your Bridegroom. Your fruits, produced by Him, emit an

III. Intimacy Communicated (3:6 – 5:1)

odor of sweetness to Him and all His guests that He brings into your "garden."

"A fountain of gardens, a well of living waters, and streams from Lebanon" (4:15). He is saying that you are a fountain of many gardens. You are multiplied many times over as you live unto Him. You are said to be a "well." A well is a storage place for fresh water. I remember, as a small boy, the well we had on our farm. We let down the old wooden bucket and pulled up the fresh, cool water to drink. Sometimes we refused the dipper and drank from the bucket itself, enjoying the refreshing water as some of it spilled down our fronts on those hot, summer days. What refreshment we enjoyed at that old well. No other drink can shake your thirst, when you are really thirsty, as cold, clear, clean water. You are a well of living waters, and when He brings His guests to you, they drink of Him from you, for He is the well of Living Water. You are being used of Him to bring life to others. Isaiah 12:3: *"Therefore with joy shall ye draw water out of the wells of salvation."* All of us who have been saved should be "wells" of salvation. As long as you live, many will come by His direction to drink of His salvation through you. All the spiritual refreshment that flows to believers today *must* flow through people just like you by the precious Spirit of God. These waters of life are called *"streams from Lebanon."* From the high places with Him come the revelations, the experiences, and the Words of Life that save their spirits, souls and lives.

THE LIFE OF LOVE (4:16)

"Awake, O north wind; and come, thou south; blow upon my garden, that the spices thereof may flow out. Let my beloved come into His garden, and eat His pleasant fruits" (4:16). This is your cry and response to His love.

There are two aspects in your cry of love. You call for the north wind to blow in a cold, frosty, and penetrating fashion upon your "garden." You cry also for the south wind to come with its mild, warm, pleasant, and gentle breezes. I believe the interpretation is this: You have arrived at the place of spiritual growth where you are dedicated to pleasing the Lord, regardless of circumstances. Your main purpose in life now, and your deep desire above all else, is to bring forth fruit for Him, so that He may be pleasured and give of His fruit in you to others that they may be blessed.

Whether by cold, unpleasant, and even trying circumstances in life, or by those most pleasant experiences, your desire is for Him to be pleased. Let the events of life come from either direction and blow on your garden. The blowing of these winds of adversity or winds of blessing will only enhance the odor of a sweet smell in the nostrils of your Lord and His guests. You are no longer a slave to circumstances but take the humble servant's place to bless Him and others. As Paul, you can say, *"I know both how to be abased, and I know how to abound: everywhere and in all things I am instructed both to be full, and to be hungry, both to abound and to suffer need"* (Philippians 4:12). Say with Paul as he speaks in

Philippians 1:20, *"... so now also Christ shall be magnified in my body, whether it be by life, or by death."* Situations and events merely develop the fragrance of your garden. All the fruits with their odors and tastes are His fruits through you for Himself and others He has chosen to partake. You are His garden of blessing!

THE LORD RESPONDS (5:1)

"I am come into my garden, my sister, my spouse: I have gathered my myrrh with my spice; I have eaten my honeycomb with my honey; I have drunk my wine with my milk: eat, O friends; drink, yea, drink abundantly, O beloved" (5:1). Notice the Lord's emphasis on the personal, possessive word *"my."* MY garden, MY sister, MY spouse, MY myrrh, MY spice, MY honeycomb, MY honey, MY wine, and MY milk! When you first came to the Lord for His salvation, you probably did not realize that from that second on, you belonged to Him. You were purchased by His blood for all time and eternity. You are the Lord's personal love. You belong to Him, and you are His possession!

However, self-satisfaction is a barrier to His claiming what is rightfully His. The words, "Most High," as noted before, mean "Possessor." Many of His blood-bought children, sad to say, He does not possess. When you are possessed by Him, you have reached the epitome of personal Christianity. Your dedication to Him is not in order to receive from Him but to give to Him what He rightfully deserves—you. Yes, all of you!

Others, by His invitation, eat of your fruit, but God alone receives the fruit of your life first. The fruit you carry, as a branch on His vine, is for Him first. Then others are called to the banquet. I repeat, for the sake of emphasis, that you are His garden now. The gifts and fruits are all His and for Him first. Others come to you through the leadership of the Holy Spirit and eat and are nourished spiritually because you are the garden of the Bridegroom. The fruit of the Spirit in Galatians 5:22-23 are all for Him first, although we have not been taught that way, for the most part. I stress this point over and over for your edification. You, your gifts, your fruit, your life, your *all* are for Him first. Keep this in mind and many problems will be avoided by you in your living in and for Him.

IV. Intimacy Concentrated
(Forming [Transforming] Love)
Song of Solomon 5:2 – 7:13

THE CONTINUING CHALLENGE (5:2 – 6:13)

THE CALL. *"I sleep, but my heart waketh: it is the voice of my beloved that knocketh, saying, Open to me, my sister, my love, my dove, my undefiled: for my head is filled with dew, and my locks with the drops of the night"* (5:2). You sleep with a wonderful knowledge of His love. You are resting in Him, content and relaxed. However, your spirit, or heart, is awake. There is much meditation about Him, your Love. Outwardly calm, most of the people do not know what is going on inside of you. You are excited about Him. You want to run and shout and dance before the Lord. Galatians 2:20 is your experience, where it is stated, *"I am crucified with Christ; nevertheless I live; yet not I, but Christ liveth in me: and the life which I now live in the flesh I live by the faith of the Son of God, who loved me, and gave Himself for me."* You have the awesome ability to let Him enter your *"garden"* or to keep Him out.

Why is the Lord calling you? Because there lies before you a deeper and more meaningful revelation of Him. You hear

Him stand at your heart's door and knock and call your name as in Revelation 3:20: *"Behold, I stand at the door, and knock: if any man hear my voiee, and open the door, I will come in to him, and will sup with him, and he with me."* This seems to be confusing. You know He lives inside of you, in your spirit; yet, here He comes from the outside wanting entrance. He says, *"My head is filled with dew, and my locks with the drops of the night."* He is portraying His Gethsemane agony. Each experience with the Lord, each revelation, comes with His approach from "outside" of yourself.

Now you are facing another facet of the risen Lord. You must see Him in several different perspectives if you are to know Him in the intimacy He desires. In Gethsemane, His head was covered with dew and His hair with the night moisture. Look at Luke 22:44: *"And being in an agony He prayed more earnestly: and His sweat was as it were great drops of blood falling down to the ground."* The Lord is calling you to a deeper understanding of His agony for you and for the world.

Why are we satisfied with where we are in our relationship with the Lord? Why do we suppose we have "arrived" at a certain point along life's journey? You will never reach a point where you have "arrived," where there is no more learning of Him, no fresh experiences with Him. There is constant revelation going on with the one who walks with the Lord.

Recall that, as He was on the cross, He cried unto the Father, *"... why hast thou forsaken me?"* He was smitten, stricken, and abandoned for you. That is the state of all who do not know the Lord. What agony He suffered.

Now He cries to you: *"Open to me."* It is your choice if you wish to go deeper with Him in this vital depth of the cross. We are prone to run to victory all the time and refuse to take time to walk with Him in the experience of death to the self-life. Remember that your identification with Christ is always based on the cross. You have received Him as King of kings and Lord of lords. Now receive Him as a *"man of sorrows, and aquainted with grief"* (Isaiah 53:3). Here, again, we find Philippians 3: *"… conformable unto His death."*

There is no pressure or force to compel you to enter this realm with Him. He calls you with voice soft and tender, for He knows that there is shame in this experience. It is hard to understand, and I hesitate to enter this realm of meditation. However, every person that has been used of God in a mighty way has had to face four experiences, in some measure, that the Lord faced.

There is the wilderness time, when you are tested to submit to the world and its ideas. Some of this will be in the religious realm, especially. Adapt, conform, and cooperate, they say, in order to be received. This is true temptation, I assure you. If you go your own way with the Lord, you will suffer humiliation at the hands of the religious crowd. They will blackmail you, blackball you, or blackjack you to force submission to their religious ideas. The Scripture tells us that they will even kill you, thinking they are doing God a service

(John 16:2). The world, also, will beckon you to follow its prerogatives and place things of its nature first before being "religious." To some extent, you will face all three of the temptations Jesus faced.

The second experience will be when you find yourself on top of the mountain of ecstatic experience. There you will wish to remain. You, like Peter, will desire to build "three tabernacles" and camp there. You will not want to go back down the mountain of life to a cross of some sort for the benefit of others. You will desire to remain in that glorious place, where all is beautiful, quiet, and good. There you speak with the Father and never want to "go back" to reality. Paul had some of the same type experiences when he was *"caught up"* and saw *"unspeakable things"* (2 Corinthians 12:2-4). Here will be a real test of your resolve to do exactly what your Lord tells you to do.

The third experience will be when you face your own personal Gethsemane. There you will plead with the Father for release and relief from something He wants you to do that will cost you everything. Then you will surrender and say, as did Jesus, *"… not my will, but thine, be done"* (Luke 22:42). There you will have found victory.

The fourth experience you will face will be fatal to "self." It is the time of facing the cross and being *"crucified with Christ"* (Galatians 2:20; 5:24). Here you will literally die to all people and things except the Lord. You will present yourself to Him for whatever He desires, and you will turn your back on all selfish pursuits just for being with Him.

You will experience these times in different degrees and times. Therefore, you will be unable to compare experiences with other wayfarers. The shame, the personal shame, you will experience will cause you to hesitate. His cry, *"Open to me,"* rings in your ears as you contemplate losing your reputation, spiritual name, or fame. Many others have done so. They have been abased by a loss of their "name." They think it is over, but it is not. God is not interested in your "standing" before others. He is interested in YOU and your personal knowledge of Him.

Somewhere, dear bride, as you seek intimacy with Him, you must go through a period of testing in which you find no help from friends or relatives. You may find one, that one that the Lord will send to help you, but for the most part you must face the test alone in your inner being. Others will believe that you have been rebuked and abandoned by God, "set aside," or "put on the shelf," as they say. I speak from my own desert experiences when I tell you it will hurt, deeply hurt. You may be accused of things that are *not* true You may be accused of things that *are* true. You will face spiritual reproach and feel forsaken of God, as did Jesus on the cross. You will be stripped of all pride and dependance on self or others. You *must* come to the place where any lot or portion in life assigned by the Lord is welcomed because it is His will for you. There may be a time when you are guilty of their accusations and think that it is all over for your being used of the Lord. I know, as do you, men who have "fallen" from their high calling. However, the Lord has not forsaken them as men have. Out of the "crucifixion" of the flesh will come glory to God. If you are one of the "fallen," then permit me to encourage you. David, called *"a man after God's own heart,"* was once a "fallen" leader. Jesus humbled Himself and became obedient unto the cross to save you and help you. Whether you are innocent or guilty of accusations by men, get to the cross. The cross of Christ will correct all error.

You have had many come to you because of your dedication and walk with the Lord. They have followed you with keen interest as you have sought His face. Now you are called to go with Him in the reproach of the cross. You will probably lose that group of friends because they do not understand what God is doing with you. This was one of the hardest things I had to face in my test. I found that I had many acquaintances but very few real friends who would stay with me through the trials. Even your friends will not understand. My precious wife, at that time, thought I was losing my mind. God was stripping me of *me*. It was a painful and sore trial, but I praise God for it. You will be grateful to Him when He brings you through the testing time.

YOUR ANSWER

"I have put off my coat; how shall I put it on? I have washed my feet; how shall I defile them" (5:3). You put off the old life and nature, the old hurts and manifestations of the

IV. Intimacy Concentrated (5:2 – 7:13)

flesh-life with its worries and burdens. Face misunderstandings again? Put that coat of ridicule on again? Walk with the shoes of hurt again? Keep in mind that there are two sides to the cross. One side is the redemption side and the other side is resurrection. You have a clean slate, a good name, and a fine reputation. Now you will become an object of ridicule. You will be "going off the deep end," they will say. You are concerned about public opinion. I have often said that there are two salvations. One is from sin, and the other is from public opinion. All your past position, leadership, and experiences were, you thought, for the glory of God. All that must be abandoned.

All spiritual progress demands change, as we have said before. Being willing to change is the price of progress in the Christian life. Spiritual complacency means a refusal to be motivated to a higher calling by your Bridegroom. Fear of anything will rob you of present peace and is a pitfall to walking with Him.

YOUR RESPONSE

"My beloved put in His hand by the hole of the door, and my bowels were moved for Him. I rose up to open to my beloved; and my hands dropped with myrrh, and my fingers with sweet smelling myrrh, upon the handles of the lock" (5:4-5). You are slow to respond to His call. Most of us, when He calls, do not respond immediately. Many, perhaps most, ministers will tell you that they struggled and fought the "call to preach." It

seems to be a human foible, or tendency, to always "think things through" when God speaks. Vance Havner, an old prophet of God, once said something I have remembered through the years. He stated, "Some people are so afraid of getting out on a limb, they refuse to climb the tree."

The same hand that has embraced you now beckons you to follow. Your heart is moved for Him, and you slowly rise up to meet Him. Because of His death on the cross for you, as shown by the myrrh on your hands and fingers, you respond. There is a difference between being moved by singing and preaching and being moved by God when you are alone away from the congregation. The *"lock"* here is your own will. You are ready to unlock your will and let Him come in as He pleases. The *"hole of the door"* is significant of the entrance to your heart. It is because of His love and dying for you, as implied by the myrrh, that you respond. The *"sweet smelling myrrh"* represents His love for you to the extent that He would go to hell for you. You put your hands out to open to Him by touching the handle of the lock. Only one thing breaks down the will of any person, and that is *love*. That is the key that opens the heart and draws men to follow the Lord. John 15:13: *"Greater love hath no man than this, that a man lay down his life for his friends."* If that does not break your will and cause you to respond to the Lord, then nothing else will do it. Warnings, fear, threats, or nagging never has brought men to Jesus. You love that person with the love of the Lord, and they will be drawn to Him. Only love brings

IV. Intimacy Concentrated (5:2 – 7:13)

Christians to follow Him. His love, evidenced by His death on the cross, draws men as a magnet draws metal. John 12:32: *"And I, if I be lifted up from the earth, will draw all men unto me."*

"I opened to my beloved; but my beloved had withdrawn Himself, and was gone: my soul failed when He spake: I sought Him, but I could not find Him; I called Him but He gave me no answer" (5:6). He is gone! You are distressed. You belatedly opened your will to Him, but He is gone. Distraught, your heart pains you, and you are startled by His action. All sorts of wild thoughts race through your mind. Have you sinned? Are you "lost" again? What must you do? The hesitancy has opened the door for Satan to come with his darts of doubt to throw at your mind and heart. You cry out to the Lord, but He does not answer. As old preachers once said, "The heavens have turned to brass." Heed this thought: When He does not answer you, He is calling you. His very silence is a love cry for you to seek Him, although you will find He is not far away from you.

"The watchmen that went about the city found me, they smote me, they wounded me; the keepers of the walls took away my veil from me" (5:7). You seek consolation from the ministers and receive rebuke. The Lord will not permit you to be satisfied with anything or any person but Him. The watchmen (ministers or other "spiritual" guides) conclude that because He is not found of you, then you have committed some horrible sin. His silence is evidence, to them, that you

are in the wrong somehow. Psalm 69:26: *"For they persecute him whom thou hast smitten; and they talk to the grief of those whom thou hast wounded."* These watchmen scold you, and they play psychiatrist, searching your soul to find where you are wrong. Psalm 69:20: *"Reproach hath broken my heart; and I am full of heaviness: and I looked for some to take pity, but there was none; and for comforters, but I found none."* There are plenty of miserable comforters, like those who visited Job, who will psychoanalyze you spiritually, using their own experiences to help you. You must be *very* careful to whom you turn in days of heaviness. You will get smitten and wounded. Only a veteran of the cross who has gone before you on this same journey will be able to help *if* the Lord leads you to that person. Get before the Lord first before you go to men.

One reason, it occurs to me, that the Lord withdraws and causes you to seek Him is that you must feel what He feels when He comes to men and they hesitate to accept Him as Lord and Savior. He is still rejected of men, and He is grieved with any of us who hesitate to accept His call to us at once. Romans 10:21: *"… All day long I have stretched forth my hands unto a disobedient and gainsaying people."* There is deep pathos in that statement. You can begin, in a small way, to "feel" what He feels when He seeks intimacy with others who refuse Him.

"… the keepers of the walls took away my veil from me." Open derision! Exposed! A failure! "Take his credentials!

IV. Intimacy Concentrated (5:2 – 7:13)

Throw him out! We cannot be contaminated with this person's sinfulness, for surely s/he has sinned, or s/he would not be in this state!" This is blatant Phariseeism, and most of the Christian world practices it. Those who are spiritual should restore such an one in the spirit of meekness, considering themselves lest they also be tempted (Galatians 6:1). But these kinds of people are rare indeed. Those who persecute you should be the very ones to restore you. They will take your church job away, your "veil" if you please, and be happy when you are not in their presence. When outstanding men of television "slipped," I heard the uproar of so-called Christian people accusing and judging them. Christian leaders talked much with each other of the "problem" of these men, but I have not heard of one of these Christian leaders who went out of their way to restore them back to the Lord and to service for Him. No wonder the world laughs at our so-called Christianity!

"I charge you, O daughters of Jerusalem, if ye find my Beloved, that ye tell Him, that J am sick of love" (5:8). You seek help from the people who are supposed to be Christians. You turn to everyone who will listen and ask them to pray for you. "Pray for me" is a cry of your hurting heart. You have learned the hard way that a complacent spirit withdraws the light of His smile. God would that you were hot or cold. Lukewarmness is sickening to the Lord. So you say, "I am sick from love, simply sick to be with Him." You learned to be in control of your circumstances and your own emotions.

Impossible! The soul that is "in charge" of itself has a terrible lesson to learn. You cannot handle yourself. Realizing this, you long for Him. You cannot handle life without Him. Self-sufficiency is a sickening thing to see. Even in your dilemma here, you will revert to "self" again if you are not careful. Helplessness is the ground for your victory.

THE DAUGHTERS OF JERUSALEM QUESTION YOU

"What is thy beloved more than another beloved, O thou fairest among women? what is thy beloved more than another beloved, that thou dost so charge us?" (5:9). The problem here is that the people around you compare the Lord to other religious leaders. What is Christ more than Mohammed, Buddha, Shinto, or someone else? They compare Him to others, but to you there is no comparison. Permit me to interject here that Christianity is not a religion. The word "religion" is only used five times in the Bible and with no positive connotation except once about visiting the widows (James 1:27). There is never a connection with the word "religion" and the name of Jesus Christ. Christianity is One Person, Jesus Christ, living in you. It is not a matter of doing but of being. Christianity is *"Christ in you, the hope of glory."*

YOUR DESCRIPTION OF YOUR BRIDEGROOM/KING/SHEPHERD

"My beloved is white and ruddy. the chiefest among ten thousand" (5:10). You speak of His godliness and how

wonderful He is. He is white with the righteousness of God; He is ruddy with health; He is vibrant with the fullness of life and power. He has the glow of eternal youth, you say.

"His head is as the most fine gold, His locks are bushy [curly], and black as a raven" (5:11, bracketed words added for clarity). Here you begin the description of His divine attributes. Colossians 2:9: *"For in Him dwelleth all the fulness of the Godhead bodily."* Gold is the symbol of deity, and the symbolism of the black, curly hair is His eternal life with never a change. He is Christ Jesus, God in the flesh, *"... the same yesterday, and to day and for ever"* Hebrews 13:8. His strength never wanes and His immutability is forever. You *know* Him, so you describe Him!

"His eyes are as the eyes of doves by the rivers of waters, washed with milk, and fitly set" (5:12). You describe His eyes from your eyes of love. You have learned the speech of His look, the intentness of His stare, and the depth of His passion and compassion for you. You describe His eyes by comparison to dove's eyes because of their softness and beauty. It is strange, is it not, that "love is in the eyes of the beholder"? That old adage is true from every aspect. The eyes of any person looks on another individual based on the inner spirit of love, hate, imagination, or training. The phrase *"rivers of waters"* speaks of the life sparkle of those eyes. Rivers flow, their ripples dancing in the rays of the sun, to carry life to all they touch. Your reference here is that His eyes "run to and fro in the earth" seeking by love to bring life to all that will permit Him

to touch them.

"... washed with milk, and fitly set" shows His purity of thought and action. He is perfect in both arenas. He views with perfect understanding all He surveys, as shown by the words, *"fitly set."* Your Bridegroom/King knows all and sees all. He is omnipresent, omniscient, and omnipotent. He is sovereign, full of mercy and grace, and is love embodied. He is all these and more. Therefore, to you His eyes describe who He is—your Lord and Savior, Master and King, Shepherd and Lover.

"His cheeks are as a bed of spices, as sweet flowers: His lips like lilies, dropping sweet smelling myrrh" (5:13). Note the first part of this verse. In Isaiah 50:6, we read, *"I gave my back to the smiters, and my cheeks to them that plucked off the hair: I hid not my face from shame and spitting."* The *"spices"* of His travail, when slapped and spat upon, is shown here. Those cheeks, smitten by the hard hands of His persecutors, are as sweet flowers to you because He received that ignominious treatment for you. No wonder then that His lips are like lilies and bring forth sweet smelling myrrh. Glorious are the teachings of our Bridegroom as He said, *"Thy sins be forgiven thee"* or *"go in peace"* or *"rise and walk."* Even at this moment, He will say to all who will come to Him, *"I am the Lord that healeth thee."* You know this, and your description of your wonderful Lord is precious indeed as a testimony of His love.

"His hands are as gold rings set with the beryl: His belly is as bright ivory overlaid with sapphires" (5:14). You see His

fingers as gold rods with the nails as topaz. Gold represents divinity, of course, and beryl was one of the stones worn by the priest on his breastplate. The Lord's hands are never lost in purpose, and those hands that formed the universe will hold you and carry out His purpose for you into eternity. God's plan for you, and for everyone, will be carried out, and you can count on that. The word *"belly"* speaks of the inside of God or a person, "the seat of the emotions," so to speak. Your Lord is deeply sensitive. You can grieve, quench, lie to, and blaspheme the spirit of Christ. You must know that your King is to be shown by you as He really is. Thus, all these figures of speech show His beauty and love.

"His legs are as pillars of marble, set upon sockets of fine gold: His countenance is as Lebanon, excellent as the cedars" (5:15). Your description of your wonderful Lord continues by your speaking of His stability, as shown in the first phrase. Power to stand on godliness is the description you give here. Everything about Jesus is high and lofty, as is Lebanon above the sea. He is glorified to the heights of heaven, and the whole universe is held in His hands. Since He holds the entire universe by His authority and power, He can do as He pleases with anything and anybody He chooses. He is God!

"His mouth is most sweet: yea, He is altogether lovely. This is my beloved, and this is my friend, O daughters of Jerusalem" (5:16). You finish your description of your beloved friend to the Christian onlookers who have asked you what makes Him different from other gods, or so-called "spiritual"

leaders. You speak of His mouth. This is better translated "palate of taste." Listen! Everything from God is first tasted by our Lord before being passed on to us. You will never face a situation or matter that He has not faced first or experienced in His manhood. Hebrew 4:15: *"For we have not an high priest which cannot be touched with the feeling of our infirmities; but was in all points tempted like as we are, yet without sin."* Nothing comes to His beloved except by His permission. What Jesus says is what the Father says. He stated, *"Believest thou not that I am in the Father, and the Father in me? the words that I speak unto you I SPEAK NOT OF MYSELF; but the Father that dwelleth in me, He doeth the works"* (John 14:10, emphasis added). Jesus is the true Mediator.

"He is altogether lovely." Should I be blamed and accused for spending more time with Him than with the wine of earthly things, though they be pleasant to my taste? This wonderful Lord is my Beloved and my Friend. Oh, what a statement. You have described Him by symbol and have told others of His beauty and His grace. However, you sum it all up with a down-to-earth statement that is precious indeed. "Jesus is my Beloved, and He is my Friend," you state. He is a *"Friend that sticketh closer than a brother"* (Proverbs 18:24).

> "What a friend we have in Jesus, all our sins and griefs to bear.
> What a privilege to carry everything to God in prayer."

Blessed, wonderful, precious Savior and King, Bridegroom, and Shepherd of my soul!

IV. Intimacy Concentrated (5:2 – 7:13)

A QUESTION FROM OTHERS TO YOU

"Whither is thy beloved gone, O thou fairest among women? whither is thy beloved turned aside? that we may seek Him with thee" (6:1). The daughters of Jerusalem typify the Christians around you who take note of your joy in Him. Your intimacy with Him draws them to Him also. Remember in Chapter one, verse four (1:4) where you said, *"Draw me, WE will run after Thee ... "*? Now it has come to pass. People are drawn by His love and joy in you. They, too, are hungry for peace, love, and fulfillment. Most of us try to find those "things" in the world. But you have set an example. These "things" are found in a Person. That Person is the Lord Jesus Christ, your beloved Friend. Now they are beginning to see the light. Your face radiates with expressions of love and joy in Who He is. Oh, that this could be true of every one of us. These Christians around you know that you are intimate with Him and know just where to find Him. You once sought Him among the others. Now they are seeking Him through you. What a change has been wrought, all because you sought Him for Himself instead of what He might do for you. When you *"seek first the kingdom of God, and His righteousness,"* then *"all these things shall be added unto you"* (see Matthew 6:33).

"My beloved is gone down into His garden, to the beds of spices, to feed in the gardens, and to gather lilies" (6:2). While you are praising Him, you become aware of where He is. Praise opens the door to His presence and heaven itself. *"His garden"* is your heart or spirit. We stated this fact a few paragraphs

above. He *lives* in you, in your *agape* love and in your inner man. Since He is the Word, *"The WORD is nigh thee, even in thy mouth, AND IN THY HEART: that is, the word of faith, which we preach"* (Romans 10:8, emphasis added). He is always present in His own garden, which is your heart. By your praise, you come out of your soulish self into the Holy of Holies of praise. When you do this, He illuminates your emotions and intellect to know and feel and experience Him. Thus, you are able to help others. You endeavor to please Him first and help others to come to know Him. He fills you with ecstasy. Yes, you know where He is! He is in your heart "eating" of His fruit there, being filled with the pleasure of your fellowship. In doing that, He is gathering "lilies." These "lilies" are others coming to Him for salvation, love, and fellowship.

"I am my beloved's, and my beloved is mine: He feedeth among the lilies" (6:3). Note the difference in this statement and the one you made in Chapter 2:16 when you said, *"My beloved is mine, and I am His."* There, you placed yourself first in importance. You declared yourself to be the "possessor" of Him, and, of course, incidentally, you were His. Now it is completely reversed. He is now the Possessor, and you are possessed. He is yours to love and to cherish, to adore and bring pleasure, but He is the Owner and Possessor. Again, remember the name of God we mentioned before this. He is the Most High, and that name means "Possessor." Your Lord is to you the Most High God, the Almighty; yet, He is intimately your Beloved and Friend. Hallelujah! The first

statement was a selfish, soulish remark that revealed to you who you really were at that period in your spiritual growth. Your statement now is unselfish and spiritual, coming from your Holy of Holies in your spirit. This is where He feeds.

LIFE IN THE HOLY OF HOLIES (6:4-13)

Remember that the Song of Solomon is a picture of the development of your spiritual life. Step by step, He draws you and transforms your character into one like His. He desires to see in you the expression of Himself. You are a spirit, you possess a soul, and you live in a body that is called a "temple" by the Lord. When Jesus died on Calvary for you, He bought you—spirit, soul, and body. You belong to Him, purchased from Satan by the blood of the Lamb of God. In Chapter Three (3) of my book, *The Power of the Older Christian*, I described in detail the pattern above and showed that, as you have five senses in the body, you also have five senses in the spirit. You live out of your spirit. What you are in your spirit is evidenced in the soul and manifested in the body. *(See illustration on the next page.)*

As you are transformed by the Lord in your spirit, the soul and, finally, the body are affected. I am convinced that, many times, healing does not come to the body because the spirit has not been healed first. The healing of the spirit is far more important than the healing of the body. Both belong to Him, it is certain, but God, as I said before, has a method in His dealing with us on this earth.

TABERNACLE IN THE WILDERNESS

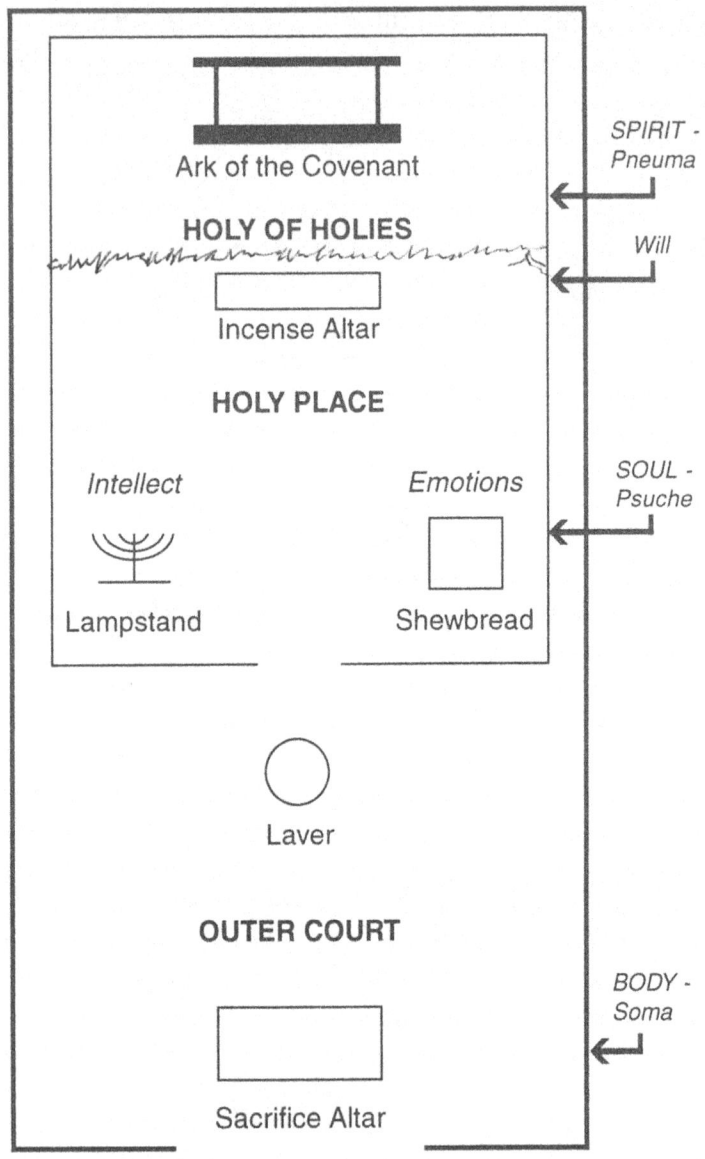

THE LORD SPEAKS (6:4-9)

"Thou art beautiful, O my love, as Tirzah, comely as Jerusalem, terrible as an army with banners" (6:4). The Bridegroom, with whom you are becoming more intimate, now heaps upon you new praise. Your personality, which is a picture of your spirit, is changing to become like His heart. He sees you in the light of the heavenly sanctuary, the Holy of Holies in glory. Your personal Holy of Holies in your spirit is becoming more like the one in heaven where the hosts of saints and angels worship the King of kings.

The word *"Tirzah"* means "delight." Tirzah was King Solomon's residential palace. This reflects where you are in your spirit, and that is where the King resides. Here again, you find Psalm 91:1. When John, on the Isle of Patmos, saw the New Jerusalem coming down out of heaven, he said it was like a *"bride adorned for her husband"* (Revelation 21:2). Your secret life in your spirit, in your private Holy of Holies, is as a bride with her bridegroom. What joy, bliss, ecstasy, and happiness you experience in holiness with Him. There is an old, old song we once sang, under a brusharbor in a revival meeting. It lifted my boyish spirits then as it does now.

> "I'm living on the mountain, underneath the cloudless sky;
>> I'm drinking at the fountain that never shall run dry;
> O, yes! I'm feasting on the manna from a bountiful supply,
>> For I am dwelling in Beulah land."

If that doesn't move you to joy, you really need help!

The phrase *"terrible as an army with banners"* is His statement of assurance that He is your Jehovah-Nissi, and His banner over you is love. However, there are many banners. His love is multiplied so much over you that fear is struck in the hearts of your enemies who are the enemies of the Lord. This shows complete and absolute victory over the powers of hell, demons, and men. This is your standing in Him.

You are living in two worlds at one time. You are seated with Him in the heavenlies and walking on this earth with Him seated in your spirit. In the realm of union with Him, you have the fellowship of your beloved Bridegroom and Shepherd, the Lord Jesus Christ. In the realm of the world, your likes and dislikes are like His; you have the mind of Christ to think as He thinks, and your power through Him is awesome. All the forces of hell fear you! You are marching against the enemy with both authority (*exousia*) and power (*dunamis*). That is why He says you are as terrible as an army with banners. Besides that, you have as many as twelve (12) legions of angels to guard, protect, and minister to you. Praise the Name of the Lord!

"Turn away thine eyes from me, for they have overcome me: thy hair is as a flock of goats that appear from Gilead" (6:5). The poetic expression continues from your Lord. The way you look at Him with love, faith, and need reaches His heart. There are two things that move God to undergird you. One is faith, and the other is love. Remember, "faith

works by love," as noted several times in this book. *"Hair"* speaks of the strength of the one dedicated to His will and pleasure. The Nazarite let his hair grow long as a sign of his dedication to God. Samson had great strength until his hair was shorn from his head. Hair, then, a symbol of your strength in Him, by love, faith, and surrender, makes Him think of the beautiful sight of a flock of goats tripping down from ledge to ledge on a mountain. They have long, white hair and are nimble and alert as they leap from one rock to another. Alive and in their habitat, they symbolize what you have become in and through Him. You are strong in faith, alert, alive, and giving Him all the glory.

Do you recall the story of Jacob wrestling with the angel? The angel, perhaps the one who had slain 180,000 of Sennacherub's troops one night, is asking Jacob to let him go. This is humorous because the angel did not want Jacob to loose him. He wanted to bless Jacob. This is the type of thing that is going on here. Your Bridegroom is telling you how He is *"overcome"* by your eyes of love. He is affected and blessed because of your eyes of love.

"Thy teeth are as a flock of sheep which go up from the washing, whereof every one beareth twins, and there is not one barren among them" (6:6). The *"teeth"* speak of your capacity for truth. Babies do not have teeth and therefore must subsist on milk and soft foods. But a mature adult in prime health has a full set of teeth. They are "twins," i.e., each tooth has a mate, and the full set of teeth is there. Only

adult, Spirit-filled Christians can assimilate the deep truths of God's Word. Jesus told His disciples one time, *"I have yet many things to say unto you, but ye cannot bear them now"* (John 16:12). God has secrets, according to Deuteronomy 29:29, but they can only be revealed to those who have the "teeth," or capacity, for them.

Bible interpretation is *not* based, I continue to repeat, on your ability as an intellectual who has been trained to parse Greek verbs. It is based on your growth in the Spirit, wherein you are no more a child but have reached maturity in Him. I know some very self-confident intellectuals who are so egotistic and proud that they think they are highly spiritual. They are, however, babies to the truths of the Word of God. Ephesians 4:14: *"That we henceforth be no more children, tossed to and fro, and carried about with every wind of doctrine, by the sleight of men, and cunning craftiness, whereby they lie in wait to deceive."* You are not a "doctrine worshipper" but have the capacity to love the Lord and understand by His Spirit the truths of the Word of God. These *"teeth"* are white and beautiful to see in His sight. They are spiritual incisors and molars, cuspids and bicuspids to masticate the truths of God, searching the Scriptures as did the Bereans, that those truths might be prepared for the implanting in the heart.

"As a piece of a pomegranate are thy temples within thy locks" (6:7). He is speaking here of your mind. You are now beginning to have the "mind of Christ." Philippians 2:5:

IV. Intimacy Concentrated (5:2 – 7:13)

"Let this mind be in you, which was also in Christ Jesus." He learned obedience by the things He suffered. Hebrews 5:8: *"Though He were a Son, yet learned He obedience by the things which He suffered."*

Study the pomegranate and you will see a multitude of seeds. This is symbolic of your mind. The love of the Lord never changes. Vital is the process of development. Sometimes you learn a lesson over and over until you are secure in that truth. Usually, the Lord does not go on to another lesson until you have fully learned the last one. As He sees the mind within the hair (locks), He sees your thinking ability in the center of your dedication to Him. If your heart is His, then as you think in your heart, you can think correctly because you have no hidden agendas.

"There are threescore queens, and fourscore concubines, and virgins without number" (6:8). Corporately speaking, His bride is one, but individual relationships are different. As the different parts of the body are not similar, so individuals are unlike. Love relationships here are compared to three groups. There are the regal queens (60), a few more servant concubines (80), and numberless virgins. These would be different in relationship to the King. But all of these fall short compared to His love for you, as noted in the next verse.

"My dove, my undefiled is but one; she is the only one of her mother, she is the choice one of her that bare her. The daughters saw her, and blessed her; yea, the queens and the concubines, and they praised her" (6:9). But one! You are the

one that fully satisfies His heart of love. Are you an "only one" that walks with your Savior, Lord, King, Shepherd, and Bridegroom? Do you pleasure Him, cause Him joy, and bless Him with your life? If you do, you are of a special company. All others could be in this company if they desired. Born of your mother, who is Grace, God is able to mold you and bless you because you are open for His touch. If a lesser work is done in you, it is because you limited your Lover-Lord. So few of us in His kingdom are fully developed. The greater amount of us have far to go in our development.

But that is what this treatise is all about. Note that the *"queens"* and the *"concubines"* praise you. The virgins are not mentioned. Why? Because you are one of the virgins. The love for a virgin is quite different than that of a concubine or a queen, I would think. Go on in grace, as a virgin daughter, seeking His face and His love. Grow in grace daily for His pleasure because He has put such love in your heart for Him.

OTHERS ASK A QUESTION (6:10)

"Who is she that looketh forth as the morning, fair as the moon, clear as the sun, and terrible as an army with banners?" (6:10). I believe those who watch your growth in the Lord are asking this question. Who is this person that walks with God? Have you ever asked this question in your heart about some saint that was close to the Lord? Have you known someone whom you admired because of their relationship with the

Lord of heaven and earth?

There are four areas mentioned about you here. One, *"she that looketh forth as the morning"* is a statement indicating that the shadows in your life are gone, and the Day Star has risen in your heart. Note Proverbs 4:18: *"But the path of the just is as the shining light, that shineth more and more unto the perfect day."* Oh, beloved bride of Christ, you should be bright as the sun rising in the eastern sky upon this dark world. Second Peter 1:19: *"We have also a more sure word of prophecy; whereunto ye do well that ye take heed, as unto a light that shineth in a dark place, until the day dawn, and the Day Star arise in your hearts."* This is how the daughters of Jerusalem see you now. The shadows are gone from your face, and they see the light of the wonderful love of Christ.

The second area describes your bearing and countenance. *"... fair as the moon ..."* describes your soft and gentle way in the world's dark night wherein you shed a radiance on the lostness of mankind that makes them raise their heads and look up to heaven, if only for a few seconds. You are a testimony of heaven.

The third area speaks of your being *"clear as the sun."* You are a bright witness of the glorious Christ, and there are no clouds of doubt, no despair to shadow your testimony.

The fourth area has the daughters speaking of you as *"terrible as an army with banners."* They see in you the signs of victory as a triumph over the enemies of Christ and the cross. The banner over you is titled *Jehovah-Nissi*. The Lord is with you in victory and love. Let me now ask you this question: Is this your image to others?

YOU SPEAK (6:11-12)

"I went down into the garden of nuts to see the fruits of the valley, and to see whether the vine flourished and the pomegranates budded" (6:11). This passage points to the fact that there are some things about the Lord and the Word of God that, like a nut, are hard to "crack." The meat is sweet, but the shell is hard. Look at 2 Peter 3:15-16: *"And account that the longsuffering of our Lord is salvation; even as our beloved brother Paul also according to the wisdom given unto him hath written unto you; As also in all his epistles, speaking in them of these things; in WHICH ARE SOME THINGS HARD TO BE UNDERSTOOD, which they that are unlearned and unstable wrest, as they do also the other scriptures, unto their own destruction"* (emphasis added). There are some Scriptures that you must pray over and await His revelation, so that the hard shell of intellectualism is cracked, and the Holy Spirit gives to you the "sweet meat" of the truth. Nuts, vines, pomegranates, and other "fruits" are found in His garden. Remember that *you* are His garden. Check your heart for His fruits. See if His vine in you is flourishing and His pomegranates of revelation ideas from His wisdom are growing in you, for His pleasure.

"Or ever I was aware, my soul made me like the chariots "of Amminadib" (6:12). The name "Amminadib means "people of liberality." The man by that same name was like

Jehu that raced his chariots at a rapid pace. All of this has a meaning for us. You were not even conscious that your soul, with its will, intellect, and emotions, raced with your spirit for the Lord. The meaning is that you are of a willing heart. He has you as a willing vessel for His movements. You will literally race to do His will for His pleasure.

Psalm 110:3: *"Thy people shall be willing in the day of Thy power, in the beauty of holiness from the womb of the morning: thou hast the dew of thy youth."* By His power, you are willing to run. You are one of the remnant. Your youth, regardless of your chronological age, is being renewed as the eagle's. Psalm 103:5: *"Who satisfieth thy mouth with good things; so that thy youth is renewed like the eagle's."* Your soul, filled with the Spirit, has renewed your youthful outlook on life, and youthful energy has become yours because you are feeding on His Word. You were not aware of that in your intellect and emotions, but it was being done by Him nevertheless. What a wonderful Savior and Lord is ours!

CRY OF THE CHRISTIAN FRIENDS (6:13)

"Return, return, O Shulamite; return, return, that we may look upon thee. What will ye see in the Shulamite? As it were the company of two armies" (6:13). This is the speech of the daughters of Jerusalem, your Christian friends that have been watching you as you progress with the Lord in His drawing you to Himself. You have gone beyond their ability to understand you. The word "Shulamite" means "a person of

peace." You now represent Jehovah-Shalom, the God of Peace, and Jesus Christ, the Prince of Peace. The Christian brothers and sisters demand that you reveal yourself to them. Those less mature in Christ need your help. They are like a fast chariot going on from victory to victory, progressively riding in the chariots of your Lord. The people of God want your secret.

There are two groups manifested in this passage. One wants to know how to seek Him for Himself, as you have done. Then there are those who want the fellowship and victory you have, but by a shortcut and an easy path. We in America have been raised on "instant" food. The "I want this, and I want it now" syndrome has pervaded the church. Instant growth and instant success is the cry of our time. Everyone is in a hurry. "Instant" salvation, "instant" sanctification, and "instant" entrance into His presence is the order of the day. Easy "believe-ism" is ours, and instant prayer demands instant answers, it seems. What an unholy lot we are! It does not work that way at all. You have come through some trying times, and if your friends are to find the same answers that you have found, they must seek Him for themselves.

The word "company" is translated "Mahanaim." It refers to Genesis 32:2: *"And when Jacob saw them [two angels], he said, This is God's host: and he called the name of that place Mahanaim"* (bracketed words added for clarity).

Jacob wrestled with the angel that he met on his way to face Esau. He was met by two angels that danced in victory.

That is the real meaning of the word. The last part of this 12th verse should read, *"As upon a dance before two armies,"* which means, *"As a dance of Mahanaim."* Exodus 15:20 states that Miriam danced with the women in a victory dance after crossing the Red sea. First Samuel 18:6 shows the women dancing as Saul returns in victory. David danced before the Lord as the Ark was brought to its rightful resting place. The dance is an expression of victory in the Word of God. It also represents a witness or testimony. This passage could therefore read, *"What will you see in the Shulamite? As it were, a testimony in the dance of victory before two armies."* You have come through deserts of depression, mountains of difficulty, valleys of distress and forests of accusations. Yet, the angelic armies surround you as hosts of angels dance in victory over your continued desire to follow and be with your Love, Jesus Christ the Lord.

THE DEEP WORK OF GOD IN YOU (7:1-9)
THE SONG OF VICTORY (7:1-5)

Here are the words of this beautiful song to which the angels dance: *"How beautiful are thy feet with shoes, O prince's daughter! the joints of thy thighs are like jewels, the work of the hands of a cunning workman"* (7:1). The daughters of Jerusalem now speak to you. They acknowledge that you are of a royal bloodline when they say, *"O prince's daughter."* The King is your Father; the Elder Brother is your brother (He calls you "sister," remember) and the third One of the Godhead is the Holy Spirit who lives within your spirit. You are of a royal line of the King of kings.

They speak of your beautiful feet with shoes, which means you are shod with the Gospel of Peace of Ephesians 6:15, *"And your feet shod with the preparation of the gospel of peace."*

They note that *the joints of your thighs are like jewels.* This denotes the work of evangelism and edification to others. *"Thighs"* speak of the strength and power of your witness. The thigh is the strong muscle of the upper leg. Jacob's thigh was struck by the angel in Genesis 32:25, and that sinew shrunk so that he limped all the remainder of his life. Strength is derived only from God, and that strength is a *"jewel"* to be seen of all. The Lord is a *"cunning workman"* with *"skilled hands"* indeed. Just look what He has done in your life.

"Thy navel [body] is like a round goblet, which wanteth not liquor [mixed wine]: thy belly is like a heap of wheat set about with lilies" (7:2, bracketed words added for clarity). These figures of speech tell us of what you are inwardly. Your body is the temple of the Holy Spirit, and so you are not in need of *"mixed wine."* Recall Ephesians 5:18: *"And be not drunk with wine, wherein is excess; but befilled with the Spirit."* You have learned how to partake of His life in you by the Holy Spirit because you know that your body is His temple (1 Corinthians 6:19-20). You have no "want" in this area. Your *"belly,"* or abdomen, speaks of the witness you

IV. Intimacy Concentrated (5:2 – 7:13)

have in the midst of the *"lilies,"* who are the saints of God.

"Thy two breasts are like two young roes that are twins" (7:3). A carnal, untaught, and unspiritual Christian would rebel at such language, saying it is pornographic. How little they know of the things of God. I spoke of this earlier in this book. However, I shall reiterate, for emphasis, on this most important meaning of the spiritual life. Your maturity is such that you feed others from your "breasts" of faith and love. You must remember that Galatians 5:6 gives us the answer to this symbol. *"For in Jesus Christ neither circumcision availeth anything, nor uncircumcisison; BUT FAITH WHICH WORKETH BY LOVE"* (emphasis added). I repeat that the "breastplate" of righteousness is faith and love. God is known as El-Shaddai, which means "the full-breasted one." He feeds us at His breasts of faith and love. You, in turn, feed others of His faith and love found in you. Faith and love are "twins" and must be of the same size. You cannot have more faith than love or more love than faith. God is love, and God is faith. We live from both. His love is in us, and we live *"... by the faith of the Son of God, who loved me, and gave Himself for me"* (Galatians 2:20).

"Thy neck is as a tower of ivory; thine eyes like the fishpools in Heshbon, by the gate of Bathrabbim: thy nose is as the tower of Lebanon which tooked toward Damascus" (7:4). In the fourth chapter, fourth verse (4:4), your neck was compared to a tower. Here, your neck is compared to ivory. Ivory indicates a suffering process. You are prepared

to go with Jesus, regardless of the cost. It might cost you martyrdom, but His purpose will be fulfilled in your life. Your eyes are like water in a pool that is open to the light of heaven. They are not like a deep well, but like an open pool. People can read "Him" in your eyes. *"Heshbon"* means "clever," or "understanding." *"Bethrabbim"* is interpreted "daughter of a large company." You are one in a very large group of believers who have "gone on" to be with the Lord. Don't get proud and think you are the only one. There are many, but you are one in whose eyes the populace can see Jesus. Your nose indicates the smelling of discernment. You stand as a military guard at the ancient towers and face "Damascus," which represents the enemies of the Lord. You are always able to discern the onslaughts of the enemy and warn and prepare, so that there is no defeat. This is a spiritual gift that I have mentioned before.

Damascus was in Syria, and the Syrians were enemies of Israel. There were towers where the watchmen stood guard to warn the populace. The symbolism is clear. You are "on guard" to protect, defend, and warn of the enemy. I have noticed the arrogance of people who believe they are called of God to straighten out the church, groups, or even individuals. They stand, many times, and interrupt the flow of the service to make a pronouncement from God (they believe). I have seen them interrupt the message from the minister to do such things. Your discernment is most important here that you may see those who are of God and

IV. Intimacy Concentrated (5:2 – 7:13)

those who are not. If you have the authority, you may stop them. If not, then pray for the one in authority to know the moving of the Holy Spirit in the situation. Your "nose" of discernment is called to attention because of the need of this gift to the church as a whole.

"Thine head upon thee is like Carmel, and the hair of thine head like purple; the king is held in the galleries" (7:5) Carmel is where God used Elijah. *"Carmel"* means "fruitful field." Elijah and Elisha were both used in this area. They were fruitful in restoration. Elijah restored the people's allegiance to Jehovah, and Elisha restored the widow's son from death. You, too, are being used in restoration. God has blessed you with allegiance to Him and power to proclaim His mighty works. You bring people back to God. *"Hair"* shows dedication and surrender to your Bridegroom. *"Like purple"* shows "throne authority." You are so filled with Him and His glory that there remains no selfish motivation. You have throne authority. Why? Because, in truth, you have only one purpose in life, and that is to honor and please Him, to praise Him, bless Him, and give Him all glory. Because of this attitude, the King is *"held in the galleries."* He lives in throne authority in your life. You are seated with Him in the heavenlies. Therefore, your authority is given to you from Him and by His power. You exercise His authority by His direction.

THE KING SPEAKS (7:6-9)

"How fair and how pleasant art thou, O love, for delights!" (7:6). Your Bridegroom picks up the chant, or song, to you. Hebrews 2:12: *"I will declare thy name unto my brethren, in the midst of the church will I sing praise unto thee."* The Lord Jesus here sings praise to the Father in the midst of the congregation. If He sings in our company, how much more will He sing to His individual spiritual love? Psalm 22:22 also says, *"I will declare thy name unto my brethren: in the midst of the congregation will I praise thee."* He is delighted in you and your response to Him. How very wonderful to attain this nearness to the precious Lord so that He is delighted in you. O, that every Christian would reach this height in the daily walk with the Lord. To delight Him and please Him is the goal for each one of us to reach. We sing delightful songs to ourselves. Have you listened in your spirit while He sings a spiritual love song to you?

"This thy stature is like to a palm tree, and thy breasts to clusters of grapes" (7:7). He now speaks to you of your stature. The time of maturity is here. You are tall and straight like the beautiful palm tree. To Him you have come to *"... the measure of the stature of the fulness of Christ"* (Ephesians 4:13).

Once upon a time as I was seeking the Lord for His fullness in me, I was led to Palm Canyon, a barren place north of Yuma, Arizona. On the great desert plain, a mountain of rocks, huge in size, lay sprawled out over many

IV. Intimacy Concentrated (5:2 – 7:13)

acres. In the midst of that mountain is a canyon. High up in a niche of that canyon wall stands seven palm trees. How they got there no one knows. They were beautiful in their dresses of green, and their fruit hung in clusters. I wondered how deep went their roots to find water for sustenance. The Lord is saying that you are like those palm trees. Your roots go down into the streams of the living water of the Word. You live in a desert land, bleak and barren spiritually. But you bear fruit unto Him because you are "rooted and grounded" in Him and His Word. The word *"grapes"* here means "dates," the fruit of the palm tree. You, with roots deep in Him and His will for you, bear fruit of love and faith from which people eat and are satisfied. Both breasts of love and faith bear "clusters" of fruits. You are a "fruitful" tree in the garden of God.

"I said, I will go up to the palm tree, I will take hold of the boughs thereof: now also thy breasts shall be as clusters of the vine, and the smell of thy nose like apples; and the roof of thy mouth like the best wine for my beloved, that goeth down sweetly, causing the lips of those that are asleep to speak" (7:8-9). As the Bridegroom speaks these words, you stand in awe with this writer. I cannot fully grasp how the God of the universe can get pleasure out of me. Perhaps you have a problem there also. However, He is God, and He said He received pleasure from His people (Psalm 149:4). I shall not question the Sovereign of the universe. He searches for someone to have fellowship with Him and walk with Him,

as did Adam in the garden of Eden. The Word tells us, also, that Enoch walked with God. Is it not our privilege also, since Christ has reconciled us to Him?

There are three things mentioned in these two verses that we need to think upon.

First, you have a capacity to feed others from Him. *"Thy breasts* [love and faith] *shall be as clusters of the vine."* Fruit and food for others come through you. While the minister may feed us with the milk and meat of the Word, giving to us the Water of Life, the "fruit" comes from each of us in the congregation of the righteous. No man lives or dies by himself, and no man is an island. Someone eats of you and the fruit you produce.

Second, you give a well-developed sense of perception. *"... the smell of thy nose like apples ..."* Apples are citrons. They were used to revive a fainting person and had a pleasant and sweet smell. Your perception, a gift from the Lord, gives revelation and warning to those who are less endowed in this area. Many are and will be saved from disaster because of your "smell" of perception. Many a "fainting" Christian will be revived because of this God-given attribute.

Third, He mentions your "taste." You taste of the Words of your Bridegroom as spoken of in Hebrews 6:5: *"And have tasted the good word of God, and the powers of the world to come."* You have tasted of the powers that will be used in the world to come and the wine of the millennial age. You are ever expectant of the Bridegroom coming for you, and the marriage supper of the Lamb is uppermost in your hope. You await *Him*, not an event or a calendar day, because He is your Bridegroom. As a bride awaits her beloved on the eve of their wedding day, so do you await Him. This pleases Him.

CO-LABORERS TOGETHER (7:9b-13

The Lord and you together have already tasted of the wine of the Millennial days, and this causes those who are "asleep" to start talking. These are the ones who have lost sympathy with the soul life and want to live in the Holy of Holies of the Spirit. It is impossible for you to ascertain who these may be. I have seen the most timid person be a vortex of hunger for Him and say nothing to anyone. I have noticed the bold and forward persons cover with many words his or her hunger for deliverance from the prisons that hold them.

"I am my beloved's, and His desire is toward me." (7:10) Your only focus now is on your Beloved's pleasure. Your emphasis was, but never should have been, on what you were doing *for* Him. You have learned that, as you place emphasis on Him and His pleasure, all these other matters take care of themselves, things such as service, soul-winning, teaching, visitation, preaching, etc., etc., etc. You have fully renounced all right to yourself and pursuit of selfish interests, whether they be personal or religious. Your

concern now is, "What is *Your* desire, precious Lord?" Laying hold of Him for private, religious, or selfish satisfaction is gone, praise the Lord. Your possessiveness has given way to being possessed of Him. You live only for *His* pleasure, to be desired by Him, to be led of His Spirit each and every hour you live. This makes for an instant following on your part as a son of God. The highest purpose in life is to be so desirable to the Lord that He wants your presence all the time.

"His desire is toward me." A little boy in Sunday school once described the event of Enoch walking with God by these words, "God and Enoch walked together, and God had so much fun with him that, when night came, God said to him, 'Enoch, heaven would not be heaven without you. Come and spend the night with me.'" That little fellow hit on a truth that we might consider.

When you and others like you (that is called the "church") walk with Him as did Enoch, then He will come for us, and we can go "spend the night" with Him.

I can't prove this, nor would I try, but I would not be surprised if the coming of the Bridegroom is not dependent upon the desire of the bride to be with Him. I cannot see Him coming for a reluctant bride. The point is that every child of God should desire and long to see Him come for us.

"Come, my beloved, let us go forth into the field; let us lodge in the villages" (7:11). Now you move with Him into the fields of people. It is no more "my church," "my denomination," "my

doctrine," "my meetings," nor "this is what I believe." All people are His, and you go with Him where He desires and directs. You no more make proselytes for your denomination or belief or group. You represent Him! You walk with Him! The people see Him! You exalt Him!

Note that the word *"villages"* is plural. You are now a pilgrim on a pilgrim's journey into all places as He goes with you.

"Let us get up early to the vineyards; let us see if the vine flourish, whether the tender grape appear, and the pomegranates bud forth: there will I give thee my loves" (7:12). In the first chapter and sixth verse (1:6), you did not even keep your own vineyard because you were "assigned" the duty of keeping others' vineyards. Now, He and you go to vineyards appointed by Him and not by man. You can now care for many vineyards, as well as your own, by His power, presence, and love. The world is now your field. However, keep in mind that your interest is still more in Him than what you are doing.

"Let us get up early ..." You are neither spiritually or physically lazy. You are now redeeming the time because the days are evil. Ephesians 5:15-16: *"See then that ye walk circumspectly, not as fools, but as wise, redeeming the time, because the days are evil."*

Your beloved and you now focus your attention upon the fruit for Him. Your concern now is for the growth that is *His* to enjoy. Any husbandman looks to the growth of that planted so that he might reap the increase of his labor. Your desire is that others may know Him as you know Him; to partake of His love and joy as you do; to please Him, above all, with the choicest fruit for His pleasure. He left heaven, born into the race of men, lived under severe pressures, and died an ignominious death, facing Satan and hell to be resurrected for your benefit and for others like you. He sowed much, so He must reap the dividends. He is the vine, and we are the branches. He looks for the fruit of His labors. *"Tender grapes"* and *"pomegranate buds"* speak of spiritual fruit for him, not only now, but for eons to come.

"... there will I give thee my loves." This indicates the whole range of His interests. These are the places where you will give Him all your caresses. Here, you will "kiss the Son." You will worship Him continually as you walk with Him in His fields and gardens of fruit-bearing people. You are both Martha and Mary. You "sit at His feet," and, at the same time, you "serve" Him and His guests. You are now quite capable of this because He makes you so by His indwelling love and grace. You bring harmony and peace where you walk and make the "brethren" to dwell together in unity and love, regardless of past differences.

"The mandrakes give a smell, and at our gates are all manner of pleasant fruits, new and old, which I have laid up for thee, O my beloved" (7:13). The "mandrakes" are love plants, something like avocado but sweet. It is necessary to contemplate a reference here in order to get the message of this verse. It is found in Genesis 30:14-16:

IV. Intimacy Concentrated (5:2 – 7:13)

"And Reuben went in the days of wheat harvest, and found mandrakes in the field, and brought them unto his mother Leah. Then said Rachel to Leah, Give me, I pray thee, of thy son's mandrakes.

And she said unto her, Is it a small matter that thou hast taken my husband? and wouldst thou take away my son's mandrakes also? And Rachel said, Therefore he shall lie with thee to night for thy son's mandrakes.

And Jacob came out of the field in the evening, and Leah went out to meet him, and said, Thou must come in unto me; for surely I have hired thee with my son's mandrakes. And he lay with her that night."

This plant signifies the most intimate union of husband and wife. It denotes the spiritual union you now have with the Lord.

Your attention is now focused on a variety of fruits of the Spirit. Different believers manifest different fruits, and you take note of this. The "fruit of the spirit" recorded in Galatians 5:22-23 is indicated here, and the total harvest of these fruits are for His enjoyment, His praise, and His glory.

Read that passage with me, and see what He desires from you in the way of fruit for Him: *"But the fruit of the spirit is love, joy, peace, longsuffering, gentleness, goodness, faith, meekness, temperance: against such there is no law."*

Bear that fruit for His consumption, His pleasure, and His glory. Let Him eat of His love in you, His joy in you, His peace in you (He IS the Prince of Peace), His longsuffering in you, His gentleness in you, His goodness in you, His faith in you, His meekness in you, and His temperance in you.

I repeat the admonition! The fruit in your spirit is from the Lord Jesus Christ and *for* the Lord Jesus Christ first, then for others, and lastly for you. The gifts you have from the Lord are "laid up" for your beautiful and wonderful Bridegroom.

V. Intimacy Consummated
(Finished [Mature] Love)
Song of Solomon 8:1-14

This chapter and section begins with your deep desire to be delivered from the control of the flesh life. Your physical nature, with all of its imports, bothers you greatly. You realize that your body (Gr. *Soma*) imposes limitations on the spirit. The inner man is renewed day by day, but the outer man is perishing and going back to the dust from whence it came. You recognize the fact that your span on earth is in the hands of God, and that He: *"... is thy life, and the length of thy days"* (Deuteronomy 30:20). Scriptures that you read on a daily basis bother you. There are unanswered questions arising all the time. You read Romans 8:22-23: *"For we know that the whole creation groaneth and travaileth in pain together until now. And not only they, but ourselves also, which have the firstfruits of the Spirit, even we ourselves groan within ourselves, waiting for the adoption, to wit, the redemption of our body."* As you read, there are two words that stand out. One is *"groan"* and the other is *"adoption,"* or redemption, of our body. You are beginning to see the need of full redemption, and you are bothered and groan within yourself looking for His coming for His bride.

The verses that follow are based on your desire to be fully in His presence, spirit, soul, and body.

YOUR DESIRE

"O that thou wert as my brother, that sucked the breasts of my mother! when I should find Thee without, I would kiss Thee; yea, I should not be despised" (8:1). You cry out to Him! There was no public kissing in ancient Israel. The only exception was for a brother and sister to kiss upon their meeting each other in a public place or market area. You are saying here, "Lord, my Bridegroom, if only they knew our relationship as You call me 'sister,' I could publicly express my love for You without ridicule from others." Public opinion is a deterrent to public praise! What others may think or say really inhibits you, and it really bothers you. You are not ashamed of Him, and you both know that, but why, you ask yourself, can you not rise above this inhibition?

In church after church and in all denominations, people have been trained to be "quiet" and "reserved" in public worship. There is no biblical precedent or commandment for such, so your flesh is intimidated, and your spirit cries out for liberty and freedom to express your love to our Lord in the public forum. Personally, I asked the Lord to lead me to a people and a church who, like me, were tired of dead worship services and where we could be free to praise Him without people staring and whispering about our conduct. He did so, and now I am "… glad when they said unto me,

V. Intimacy Consummated (8:1-14)

let us go into the house of the Lord." I look forward to every Sunday morning when I can go to His place of worship and freely express my love for Him publicly. I kiss Him as my Brother in a public place as He instructed in Psalm 2 and shall not be despised because I do. I raise my hands to Him as the Scriptures tell us to do; I praise Him with my body in expressions of adoration; and, by His grace, I am free, free, free to love Him openly, even with tears of joy running down my cheeks. I can shout or be quiet, I can dance or remain still, I can be free to be me with my Lord who saved me. No one thinks it strange or crazy. My fellow worshippers are also free to worship the Lord in spirit and in truth.

If you are in a place where you are not free to love and worship the Lord according to your own spirit, then you are in bondage to others and to some weird doctrine or to traditional, religious spirits. You need to be delivered and get where God wants you to be for His praise and His glory. He is more important than what someone might think or say. He is God! Please do not let public opinion become your god!

"I would lead Thee, and bring Thee into my mother's house, who would instruct me: I would cause Thee to drink of spiced wine of the juice of the pomegranate" (8:2). You are saying that you will be free after your resurrection and entrance into heaven. There, you will have the ability to express your love fully. *"My mother's house"* is heaven, according to Galatians 4:26: *"But Jerusalem which is above*

is free, which is the mother of us all." You are looking for final deliverance. There, you will be able to express your love for Him perfectly. It seems impossible to love Him fully now, although He has told us to do so. Our bodies long for Him as well as our spirits and souls. That, however, must wait until He comes in His body for us and we are raised incorruptible. That day is coming soon!

"His left hand should be under my head, and His right hand should embrace me" (8:3). There, in glory, you will know His fullness of love for you in spirit, soul, and body. You will be able to fully comprehend His glorious and wonderful love. What a day of rejoicing that will be when we will be delivered fully into His presence. You long for this, as do we, and wait for it to appear.

"I charge you, O daughters of Jerusalem, that ye stir not up, nor awake my love, until He please" (8:4). You cry here to those around you, those other Christians who are watching your life of intimacy with the Lord. You ask them not to disturb this blessed anticipation. You are saying, "Don't tell me He is not coming soon for me. I know He is coming for me and soon, very soon. Don't disturb this love life I have for and with Him by negative thoughts and words." Unlike them, you are not interested in the "Doctrine of Eschatology." At this juncture, you do not look for an event on a calendar of time. You are waiting and longing and looking for Him! You desire to see your Lord, your personal Shepherd, your beautiful Bridegroom. You

are looking for a Person, a Person you know with intimate detail. You could care less about doctrine, *per se*. You want to see Him in all His beauty. This is the true meaning of "looking for Him."

PREPARE FOR HIM TO COME FOR YOU (8:5-14)

"Who is this that cometh up from the wilderness, leaning upon her beloved? I raised thee up under the apple tree: there thy mother brought thee forth: there she brought thee forth that bare thee" (8:5). This is just before the Rapture of the Church. That is where we are today in the annals of time. If it be this year or one hundred years, we are about to be "caught away."

Our anticipation is by the "hour." *"Watch therefore: for ye know not what hour your Lord doth come"* (Matthew 24:42). We do not look at the year nor the century. Our anticipation is this: "Perhaps this very hour my precious Bridegroom will come for me." It is not that you desire to escape this existence with all its problems; nor is it that you desire to depart a sickly body; nor is it that you do not want to go through the throes of death. You are positive in this matter. All you want is to see Him and be with Him whom you love. His coming is a very, very personal thing to you.

This is the second reference to your *"coming up from the wilderness."* The first incident was in Chapter three, verse six (3:6) and concerned union with Him. This time, however, when someone asks you who you are, the answer is that you are coming up from the wilderness of spiritual wanderings. Through the trials of the wilderness, you have been brought closer to your Lord. Like Enoch, you walk closer and closer until He comes. You are leaning on Jesus. That old song states, "Leaning on Jesus, leaning on Jesus; safe and secure from all alarms. Leaning on Jesus, leaning on Jesus, I'm leaning on the everlasting arms." The longer the walk, the closer His appearing, the less the world makes any difference.

The world rejects Him, both in doctrine and in actuality. Most of the organized "church" is indifferent to Him on a very personal basis, and you realize that salvation, sanctification, justification, and redemption are a very personal and private matter.

The Lord says, *"I raised you up."* The citron (apple) tree is a figure of the fullness of His love and grace. His grace is sweet, an odor pleasant, and life-sustaining. From heaven (mother) you were born again by the Father, Son, and Holy Spirit. Your salvation, now and forever, started in eternity, and grace was the basis of it all. So, lean on Him, beloved saint of God. He and He alone can sustain you. He knew you from before the foundation of the world. He brought you into this earth, convicted you of sin, saved you, set you apart for Himself and will deliver you safely back to your "mother," the heavenly home. Praise His wonderful Name!

"Set me as a seal upon thine heart, as a seal upon thine arm: for love is strong as death; jealousy is cruel as the grave: the coals thereof are coals of fire, which hath a most vehement

V. Intimacy Consummated (8:1-14)

flame" (8:6). The heart is the seat of love, and the arm represents strength. All your hope for this life and the next rests on being "sealed" in His heart of love and kept by His arm of strength. Second Timothy 2:19: *"Nevertheless the foundation of God standeth sure, having this seal. The Lord knoweth them that are His. And, let everyone that nameth the name of Christ depart from iniquity."* A seal has two sides, and the reference here is that the first side is dedicated to Him knowing you. The second side is your turning to Him from iniquity. Why? Because He is jealous over you with a Godly jealousy. His love is strong as death, which holds tightly the one in its grip and cannot be denied. Second Corinthians 11:2: *"For I am jealous over you with godly jealousy…"* Paul made this statement concerning the people to whom he was sent. God's love is a flame that burns out all else but Him and His pleasure. His jealous love over you is vehement. That word means "passionate, ardent, forceful, and even violent." It is, in itself, a seal of love and a strong arm against any that would seek to harm you.

"Many waters cannot quench love, neither can floods drown it: If a man would give all the substance of his house for love, it would utterly be contemned" (8:7). There are many enemies that come against your love for Him. Since love is like a flame, the enemies know how to "quench" that love. In fact, they will bring floods to drown it. Every facet of life will be used to quench, or drown, your love for the Lord. His love for you remains the same. Most of us, however,

experience degrees of love for Him and each other. So Satan will fight this area with all his strength. Here is the promise of God to you: Satan's forces cannot quench God's love for you nor drown out His watchcare by floods of adversity. Read 1 Corinthians 13 several times for emphasis on this point.

Another thing to consider is that you cannot buy this love. The word *"contemned"* means "scorned or despised." To try to purchase or buy the love of your Bridegroom is scorned and despised. Not only is it impossible, but it is wrong to even try to bargain with the Lord for His love. You cannot buy it with whining, crying, pleading, or being pitiful. It is amazing how many of us seek to "manipulate" God into answering our prayers through some method such as pity. He is not human to respond to such maneuvers. God's love is pure, steadfast, and unquenchable. Love is God Himself and God Himself is Love. If you could quench God's love, you could quench God Himself. The one and only thing that moves God is Faith that works by Love.

"We have a little sister, and she hath no breasts: what shall we do for our sister in the day when she shall be spoken for?" (8:8). Here, you are asking about those believers, one by one, who are immature. Young believers are everywhere. You are concerned for your "little sister" when the day comes that she shall meet her Bridegroom, the Lord Jesus Christ. The day will come when the Lord will speak for her and call her to follow Him as He did with you. Your concern is deep, and you ask Him about her. She has no *"breasts."* This means, of

V. Intimacy Consummated (8:1-14)

course, that she has little or no faith and little or no love for the Lord. There are multitudes who are "sisters," saved by grace but so immature. What happens when the Lord comes for His bride? What about the immature sisters with little faith and love?

What shall we do for her in that day? Could this "little sister" be one of the ten virgins of Matthew 25 that had no oil in her lamp? It is sad to consider the fact that so many are not ready for His coming. They are neither eager or even interested in His appearance. This is not a time to shrug one's shoulders and dismiss the question. O that God would grant a revival of love for Him, the Bridegroom, that outweighs all other matters.

"If she be a wall, we will build upon her a palace of silver: and if she be a door, we will enclose her with boards of cedar" (8:9). The *"wall"* speaks of separation. You see now that you are busy with the Lord in the work of restoration. It is the personal cry of your heart to help a "sister." She is separated from the Lord. What do you do? You will bring her to salvation in the Lord. *"Silver"* speaks of atonement. You will build in her many rooms, a *"palace"* if you please, of salvation. She will be saved from the penalty of sin. She will continually be saved from the power of sin [herein are the rooms of additional growth], and in the future, she will be saved from the very presence of sin. Remember that sin is not so much what you do but what you are. When He said in Romans 3:23, *"For all have sinned, and come short of the glory of God,"* He

was saying that *anything* that does not bring glory to God is sin. So you build on this wall of separation the salvation theme. It is not enough to get her "saved," but she must be built into a *"palace"* of salvation that others may come through her as she came through you. As a "doer" of the Word, she will bring others to Him.

To strengthen that "door" of salvation, you will enclose her in boards of cedar. In the first chapter and seventeenth verse (1:17), we discussed the house built of cedar and cypress, which symbolizes the Lord's humanity and substitutionary death. Here, you encompass your little sister's witness with the beautiful message of the Lord's humanity, His perfect and sinless life, and His taking our place on the cross to save us from our sins. This is the Gospel message, and this teaching strengthens the *"door"* of her witness for Him.

"I am a wall, and my breasts like towers: then was I in His eyes as one that found favor" (8:10). The wall on your part is different from the wall of your little sister. As a wall has two sides, so does life have two sides. You can be separated *from* Him or separated *to* Him. The *"wall"* here indicates that you are separated *to* Him and *for* Him. Your *"breasts"* indicate, as opposed to your little sister, your full maturity in faith and love. This is not to be considered "boasting" over your little sister. It is a confirmation to her that she is as you once were, but she can become what you are now to your Bridegroom. You have found favor in His sight by following Him as He has led you through the different portions of your journey. The

V. Intimacy Consummated (8:1-14)

Lord is blessed with those who "go on" with Him, ever deeper in His grace and in His favor. Although He is no *"respecter of persons,"* this does not mean that He does not favor or bless those who are obedient to His claim and call on them. Anyone can find this path if they so desire, and He would treat anyone the same as He did you.

You also are in His favor because of your concern over your little sister. His concern over others has penetrated your heart, and you care for others as He does. Your *"breasts like towers"* indicate that you are fully matured in faith and love. This does not mean you are perfect, but it does mean that you are sufficient.

"Solomon had a vineyard at Baalhamon; he let out the vineyard unto keepers; every one for the fruit thereof was to bring a thousand pieces of silver" (8:11). The name *"Baalhamon"* means the "lord of a multitude." The work of the Lord is designated to those of us who work in His *"vineyard."* Note that it is *His* vineyard. Many of us seem to feel and begin to act like the place where we minister is *our* vineyard. We would not admit this, but it is true nonetheless. It is not *our* church or *our* ministry where we belong. It is *His* vineyard, His people, His church, and His to do with as He pleases. We are but His *"keepers,"* and *"fruit"* is His reward.

The *"thousand pieces of silver"* does not imply that His fruit can be purchased with money. Instead, this implies that His fruit is priceless. A *"thousand pieces of silver"* is a lot of money. *"Silver,"* as we noted in a previous paragraph, indicates redemption. The number "thousand" is a generic number. It suggests a great host of people can be brought by you to Him, for His fruit is priceless. Your love for Him and your joy in what you have received makes you *"the keeper"* of His vineyard, and you are not selfish. It is so wonderful and so plenteous that you bring a *"thousand pieces of silver,"* or any number you can find, to this garden to eat of the fruit of Him who loved you and gave Himself for you.

"My vineyard, which is mine, is before me: thou, O Solomon, must have a thousand, and those that keep the fruit thereof two hundred" (8:12). The words you speak here are not possessive words. They indicate that you have your own vineyard now to keep. Remember in Chapter one, verse six (1:6) that you were made to be keeper of other vineyards but was your own neglected? Now, you can keep your own vineyard. You view your life, which is set before you, in retrospect.

Your Lord has a *"thousand"* vineyards. As noted above, a thousand in Scripture is a generic term that indicates "many," or "multiplied." The Master has many vineyards in which He is the vine and we are the branches. There are two forms of service in keeping your own vineyard. You may labor under law as a sense of duty and/or out of fear. The other form of service is an expression of love and appreciation. You do what He bids just because you love Him. You do not keep your vineyard in order to do your duty or because you are expected to do so. You do not pray "in order to" receive something from

V. Intimacy Consummated (8:1-14)

Him but "because" you are having fellowship with Him.

There are more vineyards than there are people to care for them, is the inference here. You not only keep your own vineyard, but there are others to tend also. Perhaps you teach a Bible class or minister in some personal way. You are "tending" vineyards. He trusts you to feed this people, direct them correctly, and love them intimately. One day, the Lord will come and reward you for your faithfulness. You feed those people from your breasts of faith, which works by love. He is delighted in you. That is what He desired from the beginning. That is what you desired also from the beginning.

"Thou that dwellest in the gardens, the companions hearken to thy voice: cause me to hear it" (8:13). I speak here of the *art* of hearing. So many listen but do not hear. It is an art to hear the voice of the Lord. He dwells in the gardens that are His. Remember that you are one of those gardens or vineyards. Your growth, pleasure, and joy depend on your ability to "hear" the Lord as well as "listen" to Him. God said from the cloud at the transfiguration of Jesus on top of the mountain, *"... this is my beloved Son ... hear ye Him"* (Matthew 17:5). Again in John 10:27: *"My sheep hear my voice, and I know them, and they follow me."*

I have had people ask me, "How do you hear the voice of the Lord?" Are you saved, a child of God, a "sheep"? If so, then pray the prayer that the Shulamite prayed, *"Cause me to hear it* (His voice)." That should be sufficient. There is no "how to" teaching here but a simple prayer request of "cause me to hear it." God will answer your prayer, and you will hear Him. His voice is like none other voice you have ever heard. Satan's voice may wheedle and entice, but it is harsh and accusing in its tenor. The voice of the Lord is soft and insistent, non-accusing, but firm and wonderful.

If you have an "impression" in your spirit, and it fits the above sentence and continues on and on; if it is in accord with the Word of God, then it probably is His voice calling on you to come and walk with Him in a more intimate way.

One safeguard is to bring each and every thought to Him. Second Corinthians 10:4-5 (NKJV): *"For the weapons of our warfare are not carnal, but mighty in God for the pulling down of strongholds, casting down arguments and every high thing that exalts itself against the knowledge of God, BRINGING EVERY THOUGHT INTO CAPTIVITY TO THE OBEDIENCE OF CHRIST"* (emphasis added). You will learn as you walk with Him to know His voice above all other voices. The longer you commune with Him, the easier it will be to hear and recognize His voice. The sheep always know the voice of their master, and so should we know the voice of our Shepherd/Bridegroom.

"Make haste, my beloved, and be thou like to a roe or to a young hart upon the mountain of spices"(8:14). Your cry of anticipation is for the Bridegroom to make haste and come for you. This is the cry of all those who really love and walk with the Lord. Joyfully, we expectantly await His return for us. He is the One altogether lovely, the chief among ten

thousand to our souls. With open eagerness we await His sweet companionship for the eternity of eternities. Revelation 22:20: *"He which testifieth these things saith, Surely I come quickly. Amen. Even so, come, Lord Jesus."*

POSTSCRIPT

May the grace and mercy and love of our Lord Jesus Christ be with you as you seek now to live out what He has placed in your heart as you have read this book.

The blessings of God be yours; the strength of His mighty power undergird you and bring you to the "fullness" of Christ in your "vineyard" as you become more and more His "garden."

May you hear His blessed voice moment by moment as you tread the highways and byways of this world.

May you be filled with His love, His power, and His mercy and grace.

This is your opportunity to live in intimacy with Him. Take it!

— The Author

ABOUT THE AUTHOR

DR. MILLARD B. BOX

Dr. Millard B. Box, at almost 98 years young as of this writing, has refused to retire. He has been preaching for 83 years, with 40 years as a Southern Baptist pastor.

Robust and healthy at his age, he is an encouraging figure to the body of Christ and a living example of the truth found in his book, *The Power of The Older Christian*. You will be touched by the wisdom and experience gained by this man from over eight decades of service to his Lord Jesus Christ.

Dr. Box travels both in the United States and foreign countries upon invitation. He and his wife, Rachel, reside in Fairhope, Alabama.

NOTES

NOTES

www.ingramcontent.com/pod-product-compliance
Lightning Source LLC
Chambersburg PA
CBHW060134100426
42744CB00007B/782